Tyria D. Jones

Pain to Purpose
Escaping the F.I.R.E. to Get to Freedom

Tyria D. Jones

Pearly Gates Publishing, LLC, Houston, Texas (USA)

Pain to Purpose:
Escaping the F.I.R.E. to Get to Freedom

Copyright © 2019
Tyria D. Jones

All Rights Reserved.
No portion of this publication may be reproduced, stored in any electronic system, or transmitted in any form or by any means (electronic, mechanical, photocopy, recording, or otherwise) without written permission from the author or publisher. Brief quotations may be used in literary reviews.

Print ISBN 13: 978-1-947445-72-7
Digital ISBN 13: 978-1-947445-73-4
Library of Congress Control Number: 2019910203

Scripture references are taken from the King James Version (KJV) of the Holy Bible and used with permission via Zondervan. Public Domain.

For information and bulk ordering, contact:
Pearly Gates Publishing, LLC
Angela Edwards, CEO
P.O. Box 62287
Houston, TX 77205
BestSeller@PearlyGatesPublishing.com

Testimonies and Applause for Tyria D. Jones

"Transparent, powerful, inspiring, and raw! Tyria touches the hearts of her audience by motivating others to overcome adversity and pursue life with grit, self-awareness, and faith. Her personal testimony takes you on an emotional rollercoaster, leaves you at the edge of your seat, and will have you astounded by the amazing life story that is still being written."

~ Erica Walker ~
The Church of Columbus

~~~~~~~~~~

"Tyria's book is inspiring as well as informative. I highly recommend it for women and men who may be involved in an irrational or abusive relationship. Our ministry had the opportunity to have Tyria Jones as our guest speaker for our 3rd-anniversary reunion. Our theme was "Breaking Free." Her testimony touched the hearts of many of the women who were in attendance. Some later commented on how they were beginning to once again feel hopeful and unafraid of being in bondage. They realized there is a way of escape—a way to freedom. I highly recommend to all women ministries, sisterhood groups, books clubs, etc., to read this book and invite her to speak to your heart. Thank you, Tyria, for a job well done and for helping others see there is a light at the end of every tunnel."

~ Martha Wright ~
Sisterhood Gamma Theta Delta

"I was once in a dark place, thinking I had no choice but to keep returning to a toxic situation. Tyria sacrificed her time and finances to help my daughter and me be in a safe place, giving me confidence and guidance while helping me through the ugly healing process. Admittedly, I'm not the easiest person to communicate with, but not once was I judged or given up on. Knowing her story and experiencing the unconditional love shown to me gave me hope. Words cannot express the gratitude I feel. After everything Tyria endured, she did more than "just survive"; she's helping others survive, too!"
~ **Jazzmin Leach** ~

"I can't say enough about Tyria since she has allowed God to use her in sharing her abuse story through her writing and speaking to women. I know through her speaking, giving, and empowering women that she is letting them know abuse is not the life God wants for them. She is also letting them know that if she was able to get out, they can, too!"
~ **Gayle Jones-Johnson** ~

"It is a pleasure and honor to know Tyria D. Jones as a woman of God and sister in Christ. Her organization is changing the lives of millions of women who are seeking to overcome their past and move forward to a greater purpose. Her book, *Pain to Purpose*, will not only inspire and empower women, but it will also give them the courage to stand tall and walk toward their destiny!"
~ **Althea Richardson, MA** ~
CEO/Founder, WOVE Inspiration

"I feel that it is necessary to empower women. Tyria's mission is raising awareness along with building self-worth, confidence, and self-esteem by helping women to realize their potential. Inspiring and empowering women is very essential in our society."
~ **Ruby Mabry** ~
Bestselling Author, ***Broken Chains***

~~~~~~~~~~

"Tyria is empowering others and encouraging them to love themselves and walk in their purpose by co-leading a Marriage Life Group with her husband. She displays the mentality of a victor by openly telling of past battles while exhibiting strength, courage, compassion, and perseverance. A believer — never a doubter — she shares God's hope. It is imperative that women be educated on toxic relationships by learning how they can be free from the chains that have them bound. However, it is most important to make them aware that they are not alone and that there is hope. Tyria reveals her struggles that possibly, at some point, led her. She understands that God is in control and of His goodness."
~ **Maria Gonzalez** ~
Lakewood Church

~~~~~~~~~~

"From victim to survivor! Tyria shares some incredibly dark truths about living as a battered wife and mother for over two decades. Her inspiring story of heartache and victory takes you on a rollercoaster ride of emotions, especially when she courageously breaks the chains of domestic abuse and steps into freedom with her children for the first time. She gives God the glory for His deliverance from pain to purpose every opportunity she gets. Today, Tyria walks in her God-given purpose and is passionate about helping others in crisis to transition from bondage to freedom. She teaches women and young girls about self-love through blogs and motivational speeches, and she works tirelessly to bring awareness to the myths of abuse and signs of domestic violence. Tyria D. Jones is the real deal!"

~ **Tanya Harris** ~
Teacher, Seminole County Public Schools

~~~~~~~~~~

"I feel that Tyria D. Jones is getting her testimony out to the women who need to hear it. Her first book, *A Crown of Beauty for Ashes*, was amazing in terms of her openness to what occurred to her and her children. It showed strength and trust in God despite facing death. Her testimonial took us through all the stages of the ordeal—the act, the pain, the decision, the escape, the disappointment, and how her God sent help. Tyria speaking on radio shows, at events, and during book signings helps to get the message out. Her leaving the abusive situation shows a determination to love herself and walk in her God-given purpose. Tyria continues to greatly impact the lives of women who are in these harmful relationships through her books. She is helping women to take the steps towards releasing the chains of bondage on their lives. Tyria sharing her testimony is evidence that God is powerful enough to save us from anything!"

~ **Joseph Heck** ~
Associate Pastor, The Ark

"Tyria is an exceptional encourager and woman of God. Her story will have you crying and laughing. Her journey will leave you inspired. Her faithfulness will remind and encourage you to know for sure that God has a plan and purpose for your life. I know your life will be changed for the better after reading this book."
~ **Angel Thomas** ~
Thomas Family Life, https://youtu.be/-4mTzUTjp7M

~~~~~~~~~~

Pain to Purpose is an inside connection into the mind of a woman who stays in an abusive relationship far too long for reasons society can't understand. It provides us with a fresh perspective from the firsthand experience of a domestic abuse survivor. *Pain to Purpose* captures your emotions at the intro, pulling you to walk in the shoes of a woman abused and broken... attempting to process her reality against all she's ever known. Through her lens, we see the internal struggle of her journey, the heaviness of having to discern perceived realities against the safety and security of her children, and the battle of recognizing the difference between the toxicity of codependence and display of love. I love the vulnerability in her story and the truth of her experience. I recommend this book to anyone who has asked themselves all the "Why?" questions society throws out there when they hear of "yet another woman staying in or returning to an abusive relationship." This book is the bridge between society's dismissive judgments and our ability to be the tool in the solution.

~ **Sheliah J. McDaniel** ~ Women Executive Leadership Coach
Chief Executive, S.J. McDaniel & Co LLC
sjmcdanielco@sheliahmcdaniel.com

Dedication

This book is dedicated:

To my Mama. Thank you for making the tough decisions so that I could get what I needed to fulfill my destiny. I can only imagine how difficult it was to face the many uphill battles, yet you continued to be strong and victorious. It is because of you that I've never given up and continue to fight. I appreciate all the sacrifices you made for me. Thank you for giving me a front-row seat to see what it looks like to walk in strength and beauty. I love you!

To my Grandmother, Alzada Thomas. You had a way of making everyone around you feel like they were your "favorite." I'm so thankful for every moment I got to spend with you. I always felt awkward, different, and never thought I was as good as the others, but you must've seen that in me. Instead of pointing out my perceived flaws, you made me feel special. You treated me like a treasure. God knew you'd show me what it was like to be loved by Him. Although you are gone now, you will never be forgotten. Thank you for loving me!

To my Godmother, Daisy Sinkfield. God knew me before I was formed in my mother's womb, and He knew I would need you to be an integral part of my life. You were the perfect person to direct me to Him. Thank you for setting me on the firm foundation of God's Word and teaching me His ways. He knew you would love me like I was your own, as well as pray for and protect me. You're gone from this world now, but you will forever be in my heart. I love you!

To every woman who lives with the memories of hurt and pain: You are not the things that happened to you. Revelation 12:11 says, *"And they overcame him by the blood of the Lamb, and by the word of their testimony…"* You are an overcomer! You are victorious! Your past doesn't have to define you! Instead, use it to catapult you into your destiny as you walk in your purpose! Never be afraid to speak your truth. It will inspire others to seek deliverance and freedom. Love yourself. Embrace who you are. Walk in your God-given purpose. Get ready to be brave, be bold, and be beautifully **YOU!**

Acknowledgments

First, I give all honor and praise to my **Heavenly Father.** Thank You for blessing me with the strength and endurance to complete this book. Thank You for inspiring me to share my story once again so that others may know they can make it and be who You created them to be.

I am thankful for the love of my life, **Kenneith.** You continue to be my biggest fan and supporter. Thank you for always loving me through my flaws, helping me to face the pain of my past, and showing me that my scars don't define who I am or will become. You have my love forever!

To my children: **Patrick, Tyania, Kieana, and Kiara.** Thank you for always supporting me along this journey of sharing our story. I am truly blessed and proud to call myself mother to four amazing human beings. God smiled upon me when He gave each of you to me. You'll forever be my biggest reasons for being the overcomer I am today. I love you!

To my **Daddy:** Thank you for always showing me that despite what we're going through, there's always room for laughter. Your silly jokes and our back-and-forth banter have made many days lighter. I love you!

To my sister, **Beverly:** You've always been the brave one. You are younger, but you helped me to see that despite the "giants" in front of us, there was no room for fear. You continue to inspire me to be the best me that I can be. Thank you for being my first advocate! I love you!

To my sister, **Laquana:** Thank you for allowing me to share part of your story. We were always joined at the hip when we were younger. I believe God knew we would need to help each other along the way. Although the journey wasn't an easy one, we made it! You will always be my first best friend. I love you!

To the two women who have shown me the value of true friendship, **Tanya and Lachae:** Over the past year, both of you have transitioned from being family to close friends to sisters. I'm grateful for the wisdom you bring into our friendships, as well as the balance you give me when I'm all over the place. Thank you both for all the days when you were there talking me off the ledge and reminding me that this is my time. Your endearing friendships and support are gifts from God. I love you, Queens!

A very special thank you to **Roland and Angel Thomas**. Thank you for believing in me and seeing the greatness inside of me. You've been there cheering me on from the sidelines, even when no one was watching. I'm grateful for your love, support, and friendship!

Last, but not least, to every person who has purchased this book: THANK YOU! I am grateful for your support! It is my prayer that you will be led to your purpose through the pain!

Foreword

I first met Tyria and her husband, Kenneith, while we were serving in the same ministry at our local church. The first thing I noticed about them was that they just exuded peace as a couple that instantly made you feel at ease. You could tell they have a great love for each other. They are a great team and have a great heart to serve, help, and encourage other people. Just as important, you're guaranteed to laugh when you start a casual conversation with Kenneith and Tyria!

As we served week after week, I found out a bit more about who they are and what their story is. To be honest, I was amazed every time I talked to them. *"Wait! How did y'all meet?" "Hold up: How old are your kids?" "Whaaaaat? You lived in Europe?"* **"OMG! YOU WROTE A BOOK?"** The surprises of new information seemed to unravel and never stop.

I got Tyria's book, *A Crown of Beauty for Ashes,* as soon as I found out about it and I literally read it in one sitting. On the one hand, it read like a tension-filled suspense novel. As I turned every page, I wondered if the woman I was reading about was going to get out alive. I yelled, **"NO!"** when I felt like the last glimpse of hope was wiped out by yet another violent encounter. I felt for her. I felt for her journey. I felt her fears. I felt her desperation.

On the other hand, I realized I actually **KNEW** nothing about the person of whom I was reading. I talked to her every week! I knew the "finished product," so I knew she was going to turn out okay! I knew a bit of her story from the weekly conversations we had, but I didn't know the depth of everything she went through. If I had never read the book or never had a real conversation with Tyria, I never would have guessed that she was in an abusive relationship to the extent that she was in.

Sadly, Tyria's past is not unique. Did you know that 24 people per minute are victims of rape, physical violence, or stalking by an intimate partner in the United States and that more than 1 in 3 women have experienced rape, physical violence, and/or stalking by an intimate partner in their lifetime? These are just a few of the heartbreaking statistics you can find at www.thehotline.org.

I, too, am included in these statistics. When I was 21, I dated a guy I wasn't really in love with, but with my low sense of self-worth and the emptiness I felt in my heart, I appreciated the attention he gave me. He had a strong character and was even kind of bossy. For some weird reason, that made him interesting to me. I was known to have a strong personality as well, and I was happy he made me feel like he was able to "handle me."

After dating for about three months, we started attending church together and, for the first time in both our lives, surrendered our lives to Jesus. I will never forget what I felt the first time I had an encounter with Jesus when someone prayed over me. The best way I can describe it is it felt like a high-pressure water hose filling my heart up from the bottom to the top with love! I was in shock because I had never really felt anything so deep down in my heart before. This love felt real! I had never experienced anything like it. From that moment on, I decided I would follow Jesus for the rest of my life.

One Sunday, we were having a conversation with one of the older ladies at our church—you know, the kind you look up to when you're a 3-week-old baby Christian, and you will pretty much take everything she says as truth. When she found out the "sleepovers" were not uncommon in our relationship (before you judge, neither of us was raised in the church…I didn't know!), she smiled sweetly at us and said that if we had been intimate, then in God's eyes, we were already married. I didn't know much about God, the Bible, or church, but I remember hearing somewhere that God hates divorce. Considering I was just introduced to my Father's love and Jesus' incredible passion for me, there was **NO WAY** I would ever *willingly* disappoint my God! So, I figured since we were already married in God's eyes, I might as well settle and continue the relationship. After all, it seemed like something small in comparison to the great sacrifice Jesus made for me! All I had to do was pretend I was happy in my relationship and, eventually, I would become happy…right? How hard could that be?

As women, we are great at keeping up appearances. We smile and say, *"I'm fine,"* when in reality, we are falling apart because life is too overwhelming, or we feel so empty inside. We say our spouse is "going through a tough time at work," when in reality, that "tough time" has lasted a year already, and you feel alone and neglected. How about when we say, *"I deserved it. He didn't mean it like that,"* as we try to explain how we got that bruise?

As for me, I got great at keeping up appearances. He was well-respected, and people looked up to him in our church. For some reason, I never had the guts to burst *his* bubble…or was it *my* bubble? Did I have to take ownership because I was too embarrassed about allowing myself to get stuck in this mess? Or was it **OUR** bubble because we were the only ones who knew our secret? Whatever it was, to this day, I still don't know why I let it go on for so long.

I was known as an assertive woman. My friends would classify me as the least likely to end up in an abusive relationship. Looking back, it started very subtly:

- ❖ Silent treatments.
- ❖ Squeezing my hand really hard while holding it like he loved me.
- ❖ Pinching my shoulder while he had his arm around me.

Those things happened in public—sometimes, even at church! It made me feel like no one could help or even cared enough to help. I took it all and covered for him, all while keeping our "perfect appearance" alive.

Being choked until I passed out, being threatened with knives to my throat, and having a TV thrown at me still wasn't enough to make me leave. Indirectly, the abuse impacted my friendships, my relationship with my family, and even my job. I was completely isolated, financially invested, and without anywhere else to go. Strangely enough, he was also the reason I got out. I had yet another black eye and was giving him the silent treatment. I chose to stick to my guns and didn't speak to him for three days—and we were in the same house.

He got desperate and decided to pick up my best friend. I didn't get to see her a lot because he didn't really like her (and vice-versa); therefore, I was hardly allowed to talk to her. He thought she'd cheer me up and talk me into treating him like a king again. Instead of doing that, she gave me a wake-up call…and a way out. I'm forever grateful that she showed up for me that day.

I didn't have a "clean break," though. My parents, pastors, and even the police had to get involved, but finally, I was set free.

Except…was I REALLY free?

After ending the relationship, I was scared, hurt, broken, and alone. And I was angry. Soooo angry. Angry at him, but also soooo angry at myself! In my mind, I replayed scenes of the past few years and tried to define a point when I should have left, when I should have reached out to someone, and what the first signs were that proved he was no good, but it was all a blur.

So, I promised myself I would never allow myself to be in a position to get hurt like that again—but an inner vow like that is just as toxic as the relationship that caused me to make that vow. See, you can't heal wounds by pretending they're not there.

With time, God started working on my heart. I had to learn to "let people in again." I had to learn to trust again. I had to learn to build my resilience back up so that I didn't feel like the world was coming to an end when someone broke my trust. Most importantly, I had to learn how to forgive—and boy, *THAT* was a daily battle! I thought I had completely forgiven him, but the thought of smashing in his car windows still gave me extreme joy and satisfaction. That's how you know there's still something—some feelings—there.

You know you are healed when you can look back at any moment and realize that the memory doesn't hurt anymore.

I clearly wasn't there yet, but I got better every day. My healing process took years. After seven years, I felt like I got myself together again. My spontaneity that was suffocated while in the relationship had come back to life, my finances were restored, and my heart was fully healed.

Or, so I thought.

I met a handsome and interesting man, and mere conversations with him would set off all the triggers and alarm bells in my mind. Being healed as a single woman was one thing, but being healed when you're dating again is a whole different game.

Fortunately for me, God's promises are **always** *"Yes and Amen!"* He **promised** me a double portion—a crown of beauty for ashes.

The man I met was not only handsome and interesting; he was also tenderhearted, sensitive towards my heart, and so merciful to me when I was trying to navigate how to love through my scars. He was raised by a single mom, and his momma raised him right! He respects women, and he respects and loves my mind, my opinions, and my quirks. The same personality traits that used to get me in trouble are the things he loved the most about me.

I am so grateful to my God for blessing me with my perfect double portion that is my husband of 5 ½ years. My husband is my reminder that God is worthy of having your heart, and He is always watching over and looking out for you. We lived more than 5,000 miles apart when we met! I'm sure God put **ALL** His angels to work to ensure I got the husband that was perfect for me!

To this day, I still don't know why I went through what I did, but I do know I don't have to know the reasons behind why things happen to be happy and feel fulfilled. All I have to do is choose to trust God and trust that He will perfect all the things that concern me. I'm also confident that God will not waste the pain.

The dictionary described a victim as: *"A person harmed, injured, or killed as a result of a crime, accident, or other event or action."* Would the world label people like Tyria and me as a victim? Probably so, but look at the following *synonyms* the dictionary gives for "victim":

- **Sufferer**
- **Injured party**
- **Casualty**
- **Injured person**
- **Wounded person**

Uhhhhh…**NO, MA'AM!** I do **NOT** identify with any of that! You're only a victim if you ***CHOOSE*** never to get up after you get hurt. You're only a victim if you ***CHOOSE*** to continue to suffer!

Tyria is definitely **NOT** a victim. She's also not "just a survivor." To me, Tyria is more than an overcomer! Not only did she survive her horrible past, but she also healed from it—and in that healing, God gave her a crown of beauty for ashes. Now, **Queen Tyria** (crown and all) is looking behind her to see if there's anyone who needs her help. ***THAT*** is what makes Tyria a victor. I couldn't be prouder of her decision to use her past hurts and experiences to help other women find freedom. She turned her pain into her purpose. I liken that to punching the enemy in his face, right on the nose!

To you who are reading this book: I'm pretty sure you know *someone* who has dealt (or is currently dealing) with abuse. Maybe you once found **yourself** in an abusive situation. If you feel like there's no light in your life, remember to look up. There is a Father in Heaven who adores you! He is your helper and your shield. Look around as well. Allow people like Tyria to help you move past your pain and into your purpose.

There might not always be a way back, but there is always a way out! We need you! This world needs your heart, and it needs your smile! The fact that you're holding this book is a nudge from above that your story is not over yet. Turn the page and start the next chapter of your life. It's time to go from *Pain to Purpose*!

~ Sarah Jackson ~
Fellow Victor

Preface

Sometimes, we think we're okay once we've survived a traumatic situation. We want to move forward and just forget about everything we've gone through. We don't want to face the hard truth and difficult questions.

- ❖ How did we end up in this situation?

- ❖ Is there something different we could've done?

- ❖ What can we do to make sure we don't encounter the same situation again?

- ❖ How do we keep from going backward?

These and more are the questions we ask ourselves while seeking the answers.

After God delivered me from my abusive marriage and turned my life around, there were still so many questions. I was on shaky ground and needed the stability that my new husband couldn't provide. I had this new life with a great man of God, so it should've been easy. I had already been blessed in so many ways, so why did I still struggle from day to day? I was given a gift that so many women who had been in my position hadn't: my **LIFE**. It was time to embrace the new and let go of the old, but how? I wanted to walk into my new life and never look back.

Yes, I had worked through some of the hard things and began my healing process, but there was so much more for me to do to get to the other side. In order to be completely whole, I realized I had to go back to the beginning…where it all began. My journey to wholeness was only just beginning. The time was now to walk the path to find the joy inside me. Only then would I be free to live the victorious life God had for me.

Introduction

When we encounter a woman who is in an abusive relationship, our first question is often, **"WHY?!"** We don't understand why she's still there. There are so many resources for her to use, so why would she allow herself to stay in a harmful situation? Hasn't she seen all the statistics? Doesn't she know she may become one of them? It's even worse if she has children. We then see her as an "unfit mother." It's one thing for her to stay in an abusive home, but how **DARE** she subject her children to that environment! If we can't figure it out, then it must be that she wants to be there. It then boils down to one simple thing in our heads: **She deserves whatever happens to her because she has chosen to stay.**

I heard **ALL** those things and so many others during the 20 years I was entangled in the toxic relationship with my ex-husband. No one could understand why I wouldn't just leave him. They saw the damage my marriage was doing to me, as well as my children. Their first attempt was to try to "talk some sense" into me. When *that* didn't work, they would tell me all the horror stories they'd heard about women in my predicament. When **THAT** didn't work, they eventually started distancing themselves from me. Some stayed around for a while, but they, too, eventually gave up on me.

It's difficult for someone looking in from the outside to understand everything that goes into a woman's reason for staying. Even after those reasons are revealed, they tell you all the reasons why none of your "excuses" matter. To them, the bottom line is:

**You must be staying because you need a man.
Maybe they're right;
you just don't want to be alone.**

I will admit that one of my reasons for staying was the fear of being alone. That is not to be confused with me needing a man in my bed, however. It was more about me being afraid I couldn't survive on my own. It was all so scary, and I didn't want to get out into the world and fail, just to have to run back to my ex-husband. The consequences of doing so would've been more detrimental to my safety than just staying.

A woman is 77 times more likely to be murdered in the few weeks after leaving her abusive partner than at any other time in the relationship (Huffington, 2014). The night my ex-husband found out I had plans to leave, he tried to kill me. **If he couldn't have me, no one else would.** He saw me as his possession; I belonged to him and no one else. He no longer saw me as an individual or a person who deserved to live a life separate from him. That is how most abusers see their partners and just one reason out of the many that cause a woman to stay.

My story is not unlike many others who find themselves trapped in a toxic relationship. This book will show what caused me to gravitate toward an abusive man. It will show how past things caused me to have no self-love and accept less than what I deserved to have in a relationship. Within its pages, you will venture into the mind of an abused woman and help you to see the emotional and psychological turmoil that exists within her. It will also serve as a resource for those who desire to understand the epidemic known as "domestic violence and abuse."

An epidemic is a particular problem that seriously affects many people at the same time. This issue isn't just their problem; it's **OURS.** We must stop looking at abuse as someone else's concern or matter to deal with. Too many times, we turn a blind eye and say they are isolated incidences. Unfortunately, we do not have the luxury to continue doing so. Our mothers, sisters, and friends need our help to find their way out of harmful relationships.

I grew up in a household where abuse was an undercurrent in my parents' relationship. I understood that this was how marriage worked. It was our norm and the only thing I knew since I didn't have a peephole into how others lived. So, when I first experienced abuse in my own marriage, I didn't know that it wasn't what was supposed to happen. I didn't realize that a man shouldn't love his wife in that manner. Yes, I saw all the statistics, but those didn't apply to my marriage. I'm sure there are many others like me. Although we hear it all around us, we're not sure that abuse is what we actually live through daily.

If you can't put a name on it, then it must not exist.

To understand that you're in a dire situation, you must first recognize what it is. You're constantly being told that your life is in imminent danger, but no one is showing you the reasons why. They don't understand that this is his way of loving you. They keep pointing to what's happening to others, but not specifically addressing your situation.

To tell a woman she should leave her home, we must first define what abuse is and how it affects her. We must show her the signs and allow her to see those signs in her own relationship. Before she decides to leave, she must see that leaving is safer for her than staying. She must see it all for herself instead of going off what you're telling her. It's not that she doesn't understand she's hurting; rather, she feels like she can save him. She can be the difference in losing her whole family and her children growing up with their father. She doesn't see the imminent danger in her home because he loves her and won't ever hurt her the way you keep saying he will. Yes, they have occasional "bad days," but do those days outweigh the times when he's loving her? These are things she has running through her mind as you're constantly telling her to leave the man she loves.

I remember being told how detrimental my marriage was to my life and my children's lives, but I didn't leave until I felt I was **ready**. There are things I had to do to be ready. I had heard about the horror stories that happened to other women who stayed, but I'd also seen the failures of the women who were killed when they attempted to run. I didn't want to be a part of that latter statistic, so I knew I had to have a plan. That plan was the first step in me getting to my freedom.

Tyria D. Jones

Pain to Purpose: Escaping the F.I.R.E. to Get to Freedom

Table of Contents

Testimonies and Applause for Tyria D. Jones vi

Dedication xi

Acknowledgments xiii

Foreword xv

Preface xxiv

Introduction xxvi

Domestic Violence… What Is It? 1

Who's to Blame? 7

Everyone's Business 13

Preparing for a Wedding 17

The Wedding Day 23

Back to the Beginning 29

The Games We Played 34

The Divorce 42

Here We Go Again 48

Secrets 53

The Revelation 59

Never Enough 64

Mirror Images 71

Battle Scars 77

Soul Ties 81

The Vision 85

There's No Shame 91

Escaping the Pain 95

Letting Go 99

No More Chains 105

Finding Me	111
Marriage is the Cure	115
Releasing the Passion	120
Purpose	124
Say It Loud	130
Queen Mantra	134
Free at Last	135
F.I.R.E. – The Cycle of Abuse	138
Resources	140
About the Author	143
Contact Tyria D. Jones	145
Appendix	146

Domestic Violence… What Is It?

According to the National Domestic Violence Hotline, domestic violence is defined as *"violence against a partner or spouse in an intimate relationship."* It is designed to manipulate, exert power or control over, break down, and mold the individual into what the abuser desires. The woman is no longer seen as an individual with her own thoughts, dreams, and desires. She is viewed as something the abuser possesses; therefore, she can no longer think for herself or make her own decisions. Her life is what he desires for it to be. Domestic violence doesn't start as him assaulting her at the beginning of the relationship. She is groomed over a period of time and treated with love and respect until he feels she is in a vulnerable position.

My abuse started about six months after my then-boyfriend and I had been dating. I loved him and wanted the relationship to work. I didn't want to lose him and, at the time, felt he was the best thing that had ever happened to me. I didn't realize this would be the narrative of my story and my life for the next 20 years.

By the time the first hit happens, the woman is easily convinced it's her fault. She thinks there's something she could've done differently to change his reaction or behavior. To the outside world, this is a ridiculous thing to swallow, but to the young girl or woman who has little to no self- love, it makes perfect sense. When her abuser tells her all the reasons why she could've prevented him from getting angry, she agrees with him. She doesn't realize he is manipulating her and has already begun exerting his control over her life.

From that point, there's no turning back for her. She sees his admission of guilt as him admitting he has a weakness and needs her help to overcome "the problem." Sometimes, we put ourselves in a position of believing that we can save our man. We think we can be his savior—his everything. We tell ourselves he can't make it without us while, at the same time, ignoring our own pain. We ignore the bells and whistles sounding loudly in our heads…the ones telling us we need to run before we get in too deep. **Why is that?**

I believe each of us has a different "why," and it's reflected in how we grew up and how we feel about ourselves, even before the relationship began.

When I set eyes on him for the first time, I was already a train wreck. I had no self-love and was just looking for someone to love me. In he walked—center stage. I thought he was sent into my life by God. I just knew he would be the one to take me away from all the hurt I had experienced in the past. Yes, I was only 15 years old, but my life had already been a hard one—one that no teen should ever have to talk about much less experience (we'll talk about all of that later). There were secrets I wanted to share with him and things I wanted to cry about to him. So, when he admitted he was as broken as I was, that drew me to him even more than I was before he hit me…the **first** time.

We call it *"domestic violence,"* but I think a better term for it would be **"domestic seduction."** He seduces her into believing everything he does to her is out of love. He loves her so much, he wants her to dress the way he tells her to dress. It's because of his love for her that she must only be devoted to him and no one else. It doesn't matter if they are family or friends. He is the most important thing in her life. He will be the one to protect her from all the bad things in life…just not from him.

We hear about domestic violence and instantly, our minds go to hitting, punching, and kicking. The thing is that domestic violence takes on many other forms, such as emotional, psychological, financial/economic, verbal, and sexual abuse. Each form can be isolated or at the same time. When a woman says her intimate partner abuses her, it's disheartening to have someone reduce it to being only about the physical form of abuse. The fact is that many times, abuse starts subtly and elevates to physical. When he tells her she only looks good in the clothing he buys or picks out for her, it's the beginning of her not feeling confident in her own decisions. To her, it's just him being sweet and caring about how she looks. The underlying thread is that he wants complete control over everything about her. She belongs to him now, and he must make sure she represents him well.

We may think that being physically struck is the worst form of abuse, but the truth is that each form can be devastating and extreme. We don't often see sexual abuse being listed or mentioned as a form of domestic violence, but it is as detrimental as the other forms. It's painful enough to have your husband constantly cheat on you because you're not what he desires in bed, only to add contracting sexually-transmitted diseases because of those infidelities. Studies show that between 50 to 75 percent of women who experience physical abuse in a relationship also experience sexual abuse from that same partner (Watson, 2016). To say that sexual abuse isn't as harmful to a woman as physical abuse is naïve thinking. No matter what form(s) of domestic abuse a woman is dealing with, it is all meant to change the person she is. She is being beaten down daily until she is nothing.

I recall when I first joined the military. My first experience with my new life was going through a rigorous six weeks of basic training. That was a very difficult experience. Many days, I didn't believe I could get through another one. The result was my drill sergeants molding me into the soldier that was desired by the U.S. Army. I conformed to the thinking of a soldier. I no longer thought like a civilian. I had become a soldier in every way. My life changed from being about what I wanted to what the military wanted from me.

I compare the breaking down that was done by my drill sergeants to how my ex-husband broke me down. My desires and thoughts were no longer important. It was all about what he wanted for my life. The things he did (verbal, physical, psychological, emotional, and financial abuses) were all for one purpose: **to make me conform to his way.** It was as if he was the potter, and I was the clay. He put himself in the place of my Creator instead of my husband.

An abuser sees it as his job to make you into the woman you need to be. The measuring stick he uses is all according to the image he has in his head. It doesn't matter what qualities or talents you already possess. If they don't line up with what he expects, then they are discarded. Once a woman is broken down to nothing, she is then ready to be perfected for him. The "grooming phase" is over, and the control factor is in full effect. His beautiful bird is in the cage, and only he holds the key. When a man decides he can and will abuse a woman, he doesn't just decide to hit her one day out of the blue. It doesn't happen as quickly as they show in the movies. It's a gradual change in his actions and behavior. There are always subtle signs along the way, though. They may look like things that would be exhibited in a normal relationship, but the difference is the intent or motive behind his actions.

So, how can we tell if a friend, sister, mother, or cousin is in trouble? What are the things we can look for that would prompt us to say, *"Yes, she's definitely being abused"*?

A lot of the outward signs that are exhibited may come across as innocent. When you're smitten by someone, you look at the subtle acts of control as sweet gestures on his part. What you may perceive as a "harmless overture" is his way of slowly asserting more control over your life more and more each day. I've heard others say that a woman who ends up in a toxic relationship is partially to blame because she gave up her power. Although I do believe we each play a part in our bondage, I don't quite agree with that statement. I believe it's more about her sharing herself with a man whom she believes loves her. It's a trust that she's chosen to give. Instead of honoring her trust, he chooses to abuse it...and her.

An abused woman spends so many years giving up pieces of herself, she doesn't realize how much is missing until it's too late. She doesn't realize that trying to do what she feels is required to live in harmony with him is causing more harm to herself. That is why it's important to know who you are and not accept less than what you deserve. When we know who God created us to be, it's not so easy for a man to come in and change that or take it away from us. We can say, *"She gave up her power,"* but it's more about him stripping her of everything she is to rebuild her into who he wants her to be.

Let's **stop** looking at the person and *start* asking, "Why?"

- ❖ **Why** is it so easy for her to give in to his ideas of who she should be?

- ❖ **Why** does she no question what he tells her?

- ❖ **Why** does she succumb to his control?

- ❖ **Why** does she continue to allow herself to be beaten down daily?

We may never understand the 'why' unless we put ourselves in her shoes.

Who's to Blame?

It's so easy to blame the woman in these situations because she is the easy target. She is the one we think should "know better." Why? Why do we put more emphasis on the fact that she stayed, instead of turning the focus on him hitting or him losing control? In almost every narrative of a woman being hurt or killed by her intimate partner, it is usually followed with all the times she left and returned to him or the times she called the police to come to her rescue.

How can we change how we feel about her? How can we look at these situations differently? Instead of being angry or blaming her for the situation she put herself in, turn it around and figure out how to stop this epidemic! **Compassion!** That is a simple word, but it holds so much in its meaning. Compassion is defined as *"concern for the sufferings or misfortunes of others."* How do we switch ourselves from indifference to empathy?

It's easy to say, *"It's not our concern"* or *"We don't want to get involved."* The problem is if all of us continue to say that, then how will we change the pattern? How do we change the way we see these situations? Our thinking is the first place to start. It is how we change what we think or feel when we encounter a woman who may be struggling in this situation. To take on the approach that "maybe her life would've turned out differently had she made better choices" is society's way of continuing to place all the blame at her feet.

We all make mistakes in our lives that land us in difficult situations. The only difference is that our mistakes may not take us down paths that lead to abuse. I often say, *"It's easy to look at someone else's life and point out all the visible flaws…the things you know you'd do different."* Instead of doing that, what if we didn't just stop there? What can we do to help our sister(s) make better choices? How can we be a helping hand to someone else? It's often scary to step outside of our comfort zones to extend ourselves to someone, especially when we don't know how they'll perceive our efforts.

Imagine (for just a moment) being in the shoes of the woman who spends **every day** wondering if it will be her last, should her abuser decide to kill her.

If just **one** person stepped up and said, *"I'll be a friend who won't give up on you,"* it will make her journey that much lighter. I had a friend like that, and she's the reason I'm here today. She stepped out of her comfort zone. She chose to help me instead of being the ultimate judge. She thought about the danger I was in and chose to do what she could to help me.

> *"Carry each other's burdens, and in this way,*
> *you will fulfill the law of Christ."*
> **Galatians 6:2**

None of us can make it on this journey without each other's help. Just because her struggle is different than yours doesn't mean she doesn't deserve your support. To say that she deserves whatever happens to her because she got herself into that situation is to say that whenever we fall, no one should be there to help us up. It's a harsh way to think, and it's not what we ought to do.

We spend too much time focused on her actions or inability to leave and all the reasons we feel that she remains in this dangerous situation. **What about him?** Why are we more focused on the victim and not the perpetrator of evil? Does he hold no blame? Is it easier for us to look at her and see weakness and not see any in him? Why is this so? Let's examine our own hearts and figure out the answer to those questions.

Staying in an abusive relationship doesn't make a woman "weak." It takes more strength to stay in an unsafe environment and endure physical, psychological, and emotional abuse. Yes, I said **STRENGTH!** As you read that, you likely thought that staying is the total opposite (weakness), but that doesn't make it less true. Let me explain.

It's scary waking up each morning, not knowing what you will encounter that day. You have no idea what you'll be faced with. Will you say something that "rubs him the wrong way"? Will you do something that will tick him off? The unknown is the thing she is up against. When a woman endures being constantly beaten down, she's not only thinking about herself but also how leaving will affect her children as well. She's looked at all her options. We continue to say, *"She should just leave,"* but where will she go?

The many times I considered leaving, there was **no** place for me to flee to. The area shelters were usually full of other occupants, and I had no family or friends who were willing to take in my children and me. I had to make the difficult decision to stay. It was dangerous, but at least I could say that my children had a home in which to lay their heads instead of living on the streets. I couldn't subject them to homelessness, so I chose to endure more days of abuse. It took **STRENGTH** for me to stay when all the voices inside my head were screaming, *"RUN!!!'*

So, you see, it's not just about her. It's also about her children and how leaving will affect *their* lives. When we tell a woman to leave, too many of us don't want to step up to give her a safe place. We all want to criticize her, but no one wants to offer the help she needs. It's easy to stand back and say all the things she **SHOULD** do, but that doesn't help her if we're not willing to ***DO something***. I know it's a difficult decision to make because we're afraid to put our own lives at risk, but it must be done. It's time we do something different and unexpected. I'm speaking not only from the experience of being a woman in trouble but also as a woman who has helped other women get out of their abusive relationships.

When we see a friend in need, we act! All the other stuff can be sorted out later. We can no longer continue to stand back and watch our sisters, friends, mothers, and daughters suffer the fate of death. According to the National Domestic Violence Hotline, 1 in 4 women (24.3%) aged 18 and older in the United States have been the victim of severe physical violence by an intimate partner in their lifetime. Statistics also show that according to the FBI's Supplemental Homicide Reports release by the nonprofit Violence Policy Center in September 2018, "In 2016, more than 1,800 women were murdered by men in single-victim or single-offender incidents submitted to the FBI, and 85 percent of them were murdered by a man they knew. Of the 1,809 women killed, 962 were wives, ex-wives, or current girlfriends—meaning more than half were or had been romantically linked to their killer" (Lissner, 2019).

These numbers show that there's no time to figure out who's to blame. Instead, our focus must be on stopping this epidemic and getting to a resolution. The first part of solving a problem is admitting that it exists. Once we admit that domestic violence is not just "her issue, but ours," only then can we take the next step in preventing more women from dying at the hands of the man who professed his love to her. Yes, we can look at everyone involved and say he's wrong or it's her fault, but ultimately, we must decide whether assigning responsibility is more important than looking at the root problem.

When we encounter an issue, it's always easiest to look outward before looking inside ourselves to examine our own part in the situation. We see news reports of women dying at the hands of their intimate partners, and we can't seem to understand why it's happening so often. Although it's tempting to look at the individuals involved, we must admit that each occurrence of violence against women is not isolated. It's a problem that happens so frequently, we're no longer shocked when we hear the stories on the news or read about them on our social media streams. What's happening in our society that this has become the norm?

Many times, when a child gets into trouble with the law, people immediately look at the parents. What did the parents do to cause them to go down this misguided path? They should've seen something in their child's behavior and prevented them from going astray. Maybe if they were better parents, their child wouldn't have committed that horrible act. What about the parents of an abusive man? Are they to blame for their son growing up and assaulting his partner? Let's think about that for a moment. Is there a difference between the two? No! The only difference is the crime for which each is guilty.

Although I don't agree with shaming parents for the actions of their children, I do see that we each play a role. I'm not just talking about the parents, but **society as a whole.** I believe the subliminal messages our boys receive contribute to their actions. What I mean by this is that we constantly tell our boys they must be strong and not weak. They must run their households and not allow their woman to disrespect them. They must present a tough exterior, and it's not "cool" to show weakness in any area, as doing so would make them "less of a man." Talk about confusion! We must do better about the messages we're sending to our boys, both directly and indirectly.

Before we can point fingers at **anyone**, we must first look inward to make sure we're not unknowingly contributing to the problem.

Everyone's Business

One of the reasons some choose to turn a blind eye to domestic violence when they see it is because they don't feel it's their place to intervene. They may feel uncomfortable getting involved in a "family matter."

Growing up, I always heard, *"What goes on in the house stays in the house."* You **never** share the family business with anyone outside the home. That ideology has caused so much grief to so many. If something is happening within the family unit that is causing harm to any of the members, then it can't be hidden under the label of "family business." The family unit is the fabric of which our nation is built. If the family structure is damaged, society is affected.

When it became evident that my then-husband was abusing me, friends would pretend they didn't know or see what was happening. Maybe it was easier for them to overlook because they didn't want to break up my home? After all, our babies were young. At the time of the brunt of the abuse, they were all under five years of age. As I reflect on those days, the children should've been the **MAIN** reason for them to step up and get all up in our business!

So, what happens when a woman finally decides to leave an abusive situation? According to the National Center for Health Research, *"The most dangerous time in an abusive relationship is when the victim tries to leave; that is when he or she is most likely to be killed by the abuser. Homicide is one of the top 10 causes of death for women aged 20-44, and more women are killed by their partners than by anyone else."* These statistics focus on the danger to the **woman**, but it doesn't show dangers to ***others***.

What about the harm that may come to the children? Studies show that children who experience violence in the home are more likely to become a perpetrator themselves. They also have a higher rate of gravitating to risky behaviors such as drug use or promiscuity later in life. The effects to them go beyond the physical and occur whether or not they are victims of abuse. The psychological damage causes a lasting imprint on their brains.

Witnessing the abuse I endured affected each of my children in different ways. We know that each child is unique and will choose to deal with things in various ways, even when they experience the same trauma(s). The commonality is that each struggled with what they saw or heard during the years we lived in that toxic environment. They were exposed to violence inside the home that was far worse than anything they'd see on television. When a child experiences a traumatic situation—such as a father beating their mother—it is confusing. It's hard to understand how the person who is supposed to protect you from the world is the one of whom you're afraid.

It's difficult to reconcile the love you have for your father and the hatred you feel with each incident. It causes an irrevocable imprint on the child's brain. The studies showing how this affects children are alarming. *"There are approximately around 3.3 million children in the United States that were exposed to violence, and these children are likely to have higher levels of hostility, anger, anxiety, and mental health instability. So, imagine this huge number of children growing up and starting their own families. In fact, male children who have witnessed their mothers being abused by their fathers are at much more risk to grow up and do the same thing to their partners"* (Kahn, 2018).

How do we prevent the child from becoming a future perpetrator, especially when we consider he is only exhibiting learned behavior and doing what comes naturally? It's his normal. It's what he grew up seeing. It's what his father taught him about "being a man," making sure he's in control of his household and everyone who resides there. Do we treat the man who grew up in an abusive home any different than the one who didn't? Isn't he a victim, too? It's a never-ending cycle of ugliness. So, something that was only supposed to be their problem is now our problem because we did nothing. We sat back and allowed it to continue from generation to generation because we didn't want to take a stand.

We've discussed how domestic violence affects the children, but what about the rest of us? How many stories have we heard about the woman leaving, only to be hunted down and killed once her abuser found her? **TOO MANY!** The scary part is that some of these stories didn't involve just the woman, but innocent bystanders as well. In many instances, the abuser tracked her down at her workplace. He had no consideration for anyone else who would end up in his crosshairs. His dominating thought was likely, *"If I can't have her, no one will!"* He had one goal: to take her **out!**

As you read the paragraph above, you may have thought, *"That is a reason for me **NOT** to get involved!"* Believe it or not, you would be safer if you **WERE** involved. I say this because if you are aware of the potential for an abuser to show up at the workplace to harm your coworker, you'd be more likely to call the police if you saw him approaching the building. Having more eyes looking out for her safety protects everyone, and it shows the abuser that she is not alone.

In the instances where the abuser was able to harm the woman in her workplace or other location, usually, no one knew she was experiencing any problems. They had no idea what was going on and saw no reason to be alarmed when the abuser showed up. That is one of the reasons it's the most dangerous time for a woman. Her focus is escaping and staying safe, but she doesn't enlist the help of those around her. Therefore, she is left unprotected and must fend for herself. Next thing we know, we see her neighbors, friends, family members, and coworkers on the evening news saying, *"I wish she told me."*

Why doesn't she ask for the help of everyone she knows? As we've discussed, domestic violence is not only her business…it's yours and mine as well. If we want this epidemic to stop, we must all put our heads and hands together to create a lasting change. Instead of saying, *"It's not **MY** problem,"* we must, instead, begin to say, **"I am my sister's keeper."**

Preparing for a Wedding

My wedding day was beautiful! It was everything I ever dreamed it would be. I remember being so excited about being able to pick out a wedding gown and go through all the steps that I didn't have the opportunity to do in my previous marriages. All my dreams were coming true, and I was on cloud nine.

As my relationship with Kenny went from friendship to courtship, I started looking at wedding gowns. It became an obsession! I knew the proposal was coming soon, and I was very anxious about being prepared. All the gowns were so beautiful. I must've looked at hundreds before finding "the one." Once I found it, it was as if it was the only dress on the screen. I sat staring at it in awe for what seemed like hours. I imagined walking down the aisle to marry the love of my life. I revisited the website daily. It was **MY** wedding dress, and I had to have it to make my day perfect.

Then, it happened. **HE PROPOSED!** The date was June 2nd, and I started the day like any other. However, on this day, I woke up sick. As soon as I opened my eyes, I knew I'd be confined to the bed the entire day. It was going to be "one of those days." At the time, Kenny was in California making a delivery for work, so I knew it would be a few days before I'd see him again. I'd gotten used to seeing him every other week. He was an over-the-road truck driver, so I knew that would be the life I would have to get used to if we were going to stay together.

It had been less than two months since we started courting, and I was ecstatic about how our relationship was progressing. I had suspected he was planning to propose soon, and I was constantly looking for little hints. I was determined not to be caught off-guard by the proposal. Yes, I know it's supposed to be a surprise, but I wasn't having any of that. Everyone around me got used to my annoying questions and inquiries about when he was going to propose.

I've always prided myself on being good at figuring things out. I always knew when someone was going to surprise me, so I had it in my mind that I'd figure this out, too. Just as God had given me a beautiful surprise when he brought Kenny into my life, the proposal would be no less worthy of this magnitude.

Later that day, my two older daughters called and told me they'd been shopping and were on their way home. They wanted me to see all the things they had purchased. I was not in the mood to get out of bed, but they insisted. Once they arrived, instead of bringing the things into the bedroom, everything was left in the living room. I pleaded with them to transport all the bags to me in my bedroom, but they refused and dragged me out of the comfort of my bed. I should've known something wasn't right by their behavior. They'd normally not behave in that manner or **INSIST** on having their way. If I was not feeling well, they are the same ones who'd bring me soup and help in any way they could until I was feeling better. I just didn't understand why me seeing their new shoes was so important at that moment…**but it was!**

As I entered the living room and turned the corner to go toward the dining room, there he was. Kenny was on one knee with a ring box opened. At that moment, instead of being happy and squealing (like women normally do), I ran back to the bedroom. As I ran, I was screaming at him and the girls, **"Why did you do this to me?"** I was so upset…and for a good reason.

Since that day started with me not feeling well, I had taken no care with my appearance. It was my first time getting out of bed that day, so I looked a mess, and my hair was all over the place. Did any of them seriously think that was how I wanted to look in the pictures? I asked my oldest daughter to help me throw myself together. No way was I going to allow him to propose until I was properly prepared!

Once she finished putting me together, I went back to the living room where Kenny remained on one knee. As he proposed, I began to think about all the things God had done to bring me to this moment. I had just turned 40, and it seemed as if my life was just beginning. The day started so gloomy but ended with me being engaged to the love of my life. What better gift could I have asked God for? He always gave the best surprises that included beautiful gifts.

The next day, I hit the ground running. I was engaged now and had a wedding to plan. There were so many things to do. The planner in me wanted to make sure nothing was missed. Where would we hold the ceremony? Who would be my bridesmaids? Photographer. Flowers. Bridesmaid dresses. It was all so overwhelming, but I **LOVED** it! That was an exciting time in my life, but there was also a lot of anxiety going on inside of me.

During this time of planning, it's typical for the bride to be on edge or anxious because she wants her day to be a certain way. She wants it to be her vision of perfection. Planning a wedding is filled with an array of emotions for the bride-to-be and everyone around her, but it also comes with a lot of stress. Sometimes, others view her actions as that of a "Bridezilla." I didn't want people to see me in that manner, so I did everything I could to accommodate everyone involved in my special day. Instead of talking to Kenny about what was going on internally, I kept everything hidden inside.

The closer we got to the wedding day, the more anxious I became. The stress from it all started to affect my sleep, and I began to have anxiety attacks during the night. It was so unsettling because I didn't quite understand why it was happening to me. No matter how much I prayed, the anxiousness in my spirit wouldn't go away; it only intensified by the day. There was so much excitement in the air, but none of it existed inside of me.

Our wedding day was set for August 4th. There wasn't much time to get everything done. I had no time to break down; no time to try to figure things out. I had to be strong. I had to put on a strong front for everyone. I couldn't let them see that I was cracking inside. Most brides say that they are so enveloped in the joy of the upcoming day that they don't have time to think about anything other than wedding plans. For me, there was so much pressure to put on a happy face, I buried the turmoil I was experiencing and kept it moving right along.

What was my problem? Why was I feeling this flood of emotions? Why couldn't I be like other brides-to-be? Was this what I was supposed to be doing? Had I made a mistake by saying yes to Kenny's proposal?

Kenny did all he could to help me be at ease. Although he was still on the road for work, he did what he could to take some of the load of the planning out of my hands. Despite his help, it still seemed like there was just too much to do in too little time. I often thought that maybe if I would've had more time to plan, everything wouldn't have been so hectic and overwhelming. The fact of the matter is that no matter how much time I would've been given, nothing would have been different because my anxiety had less to do with the wedding and more to do with what I was trying so hard to suppress: my past!

About a month before our wedding day, everything seemed to fall apart. Kenny and I were at odds with each other over little things that turned into big things. Nothing was working. We had people who were part of the wedding party canceling, and others threatened to boycott the wedding altogether if they couldn't have an official role in our big day. It was all just crazy! Instead of the stress being mine alone, Kenny and I were both feeling it. I took it as a sign that maybe we weren't supposed to be together. After all, it shouldn't have been that hard! Everything should've been running smoothly that close to our big day. After a difficult conversation, we made the decision that we couldn't move forward with the wedding. In my mind, it was a joint decision, but in my heart, I knew it was my decision, and Kenny just agreed with what I wanted to do...or **NOT** do.

Before Kenny came along, I spent years of my life allowing God to heal me. I had taken the hard steps and done the things He'd asked of me. I thought my journey of healing was done. It wasn't until after the engagement that those other things came flooding back in. I realized there was still so much I had been holding on to and so many fears I needed to release. Otherwise, I would've entered the marital union carrying baggage from my past relationships.

After counseling with our pastor and "sitting with" the decision to call off the wedding for a couple of days, I knew we had to make a final decision. If we decided that marriage wasn't for us, then some things needed to be canceled and people needed to be told. Despite the craziness all around me, I knew without a doubt that I was supposed to be Kenny's wife. At that point, we decided it was us against the world and that no matter what happened, we would get through it.

Not only was I going through physical preparations for my wedding day, but I was also undergoing spiritual preparations. I've often heard that the healing process is like peeling an onion. There are so many layers that need to be stripped before the process is complete. The more I allowed God to remove things, the healthier I became. Although two months isn't much time to prepare a heart and set it free, I soon realized that God's timing is different than my own.

The Wedding Day

The big day arrived, and I could finally breathe a sigh of relief. I was relieved because there'd be no more preparation, no more people being upset with me, and no more trying to pretend I was happy when I wasn't. I could take the time I needed to focus on complete healing. I knew I needed to deal with those things that I kept running away from.

As I walked down the aisle toward Kenny, my heart was filled with fear. I had many conflicting thoughts about this day and this marriage. I was about to make a commitment to Kenny and God. The words I would utter weren't just menial words you say every day. I'd be entering a sacred covenant with this man and my God.

My son and I walked down the aisle arm in arm, and he made little jokes to make me feel less nervous. Still, everything inside me felt like it was going haywire. I was all mixed up inside and couldn't stop the words that swirled in my head. I laughed at his jokes just to get out of my own head. I pushed down the thoughts that were telling me to run the other way. I ignored the feelings of panic. I told myself to focus on Kenny and look ahead to what my future would be, instead of holding on to my horrible past. As my son and I continued to make our way up the aisle, I could see Kenny at the front of the church standing next to my pastor. He had a huge, loving smile on his face. When I looked at him, I saw so much love. I could see safety in his eyes, leaving me with a sense of security. I knew this was the right decision for me. Saying our vows wasn't something I took lightly. I had been down this road before and knew what came after the words. I knew the commitment was about me, Kenny, our children, and our future.

When God puts two people together, the marriage isn't just about them, but all the things they will do together for His Kingdom. It's so important to allow God to choose your mate instead of choosing one for yourself. He knows the purpose He has assigned to you and the person you will marry. Although we each have a purpose that only we can fulfill, I also believe God has given married couples an assignment as well. It's something that the two of you will do together that will complement and align with your individual purpose for the Kingdom.

I was entering this holy covenant, unlike the others. There's a saying, *"Eyes wide open."* My previous marriages had been out of necessity and fear. Each time, I felt I needed a man to take care of me. I didn't think I'd be able to "do life" on my own, so I hitched myself to someone else. Marrying Kenny was different! Yes, I knew I needed him, but it wasn't the need a woman has when she's looking for someone to fill a void inside her. This need was more about my destiny and the purpose I knew God had placed on my life.

Before we made it to our wedding day, Kenny had already started pouring into me. What I mean by that is from the beginning, he encouraged me and told me I could do anything. He never let me forget who I was, even on the days when I doubted it. When you've come from bad relationships, you don't always trust your own decisions. Even when God brings someone into your life who is good for and to you, you continue to question everything. The thoughts in your head are questioned at every turn, and you don't trust what you think or feel.

That is the reason it's so important to connect with who God brings into your life. God sees the heart of a person, even when all we can see is what they choose to show us. Although we can be deceived into thinking someone is for us, our Heavenly Father knows whether they are detrimental to our physical, emotional, and spiritual health. He knows if they will deter us and cause us to be distracted from the path He has set before us.

That was the problem I was having—the reason for the stressful days and nights and the reason I had so many anxiety attacks during the months leading up to our big day. I had trusted my own decisions in previous marriages, and those were mistakes. How was I to know for sure that this wasn't another time I was doing the wrong thing? In the past, marriage had become a safety net for me. Instead of depending on God to catch me whenever I fell, I looked to a man to do it. It didn't matter how much pain I knew I'd encounter in the days ahead; I just wanted the security of knowing that someone else was there. Unfortunately, the security I thought I'd have was **false security.** I convinced myself this person would be able to take care of everything I needed.

Although I didn't have an example of a Godly marriage growing up, I've always felt that it was something I wanted—no matter what. I wanted my children to grow up in a home with two parents. I believed that being in a bad marriage was better than being a single parent. Despite the turmoil in my previous marriages, I had an overwhelming desire to make them work; otherwise, I would be labeled a "failure." Sometimes, we stay in a bad relationship instead of accepting the fact that we've done all we could and choosing to walk away. We think a bad relationship is better than being alone. That's the lie we tell ourselves!

Those and more were all the thoughts running through my head that beautiful August day. I should've been focused on moving forward and the wonderful days ahead with Kenny, but I couldn't because I had so much baggage I was bringing into the marriage. There was so much dead weight, it weighed me down. I didn't know then that God was about to help me release everything I'd been holding onto. Kenny was the answer to help me get through it.

I must pause here to say this: Please understand that I'm in **no way** saying it's okay to bring baggage into a new relationship. **Neither** am I saying we should expect a man to help us in our healing process. I'm simply stating this was the state I was in when I married the love of my life. I do believe God anointed Kenny to be my husband. He was spiritually prepared to help me heal and walk with me through the bad days. Not everyone can handle being in the position he was placed, but I do believe he did so, knowing what would be expected. At every turn, he prayed with and for me and made sure I always knew I wasn't alone. He also understood the calling that was placed upon him as my husband.

When we think about marriage, we sometimes forget it takes hard work and sacrifice on the part of both parties. A great marriage doesn't "just happen"; it takes two people who are fully committed to the relationship. Although it is best not to enter this covenant with scars, many of us do so unknowingly. Anyone who has had previous relationships prior to marriage knows that sometimes, it's not possible to go in clean. What I mean by "clean" is that the option to enter a new relationship untouched and without injuries isn't always feasible. I believe this is where God's grace comes in.

Our wedding night was painful for both of us. It wasn't what it should've been. I was combatting all the thoughts in my head and didn't know how to give voice of those things to him. Would he understand? What would he say? I felt like I had already started out not being "Wife of the Year" — and we were only a few hours in! Although there had been previous marriages to my credit, marrying Kenny was like I was a first-time bride. I wanted this marriage to be successful and, to me, that meant doing all the right things.

I didn't realize I was setting myself up by depending on old ways of thinking. Instead of looking ahead and focusing on future things, I kept reliving old things and basing my new life on relics of the past.

"Therefore, if any man be in Christ, he is a new creature: old things are passed away; behold, all things are become new."
2 Corinthians 5:17

The first step in my healing was to change my *mindset*. I couldn't compare this marriage to the others because it was different. I had a man who was filled with God's Spirit, and he walked in God's ways.

As for me, I was a new person. I wasn't the same woman who trusted in my own thoughts and ways. I relied completely on God to order my steps and direct my path. I knew I couldn't go back to that old way of thinking and relying on my own efforts. I had to trust God to lead me in every way, including how to be the wife He called me to be. We can't move ahead to the future if we're constantly looking behind us. Eventually, we'll start tripping over our own feet, delaying the progress God wants to make in our lives.

So, I realized I had to go back to the beginning. Yes, I had achieved some healing in the years since God freed me from the grips of my ex-husband. The work I did to become whole were hard years, but on my wedding night, as I laid in my bed next to the gift God blessed me with, I realized that there was more work that needed to be done.

It was time to stop tripping over the excess baggage. I needed to board the plane to true freedom in God. That was the only way I'd be able to not only be a good wife but also fully embrace who I was and walk in the purpose God had set before me. Before I could do any of that, I had to figure out what was inside the baggage I kept tripping over.

Let's go back to where it all began...

Back to the Beginning

I grew up in a little town called Pompano Beach, Florida. It's a place that not a lot of people have ever heard of. Whenever someone asks me where I'm from, I always say, *"Fort Lauderdale,"* because they **instantly** know where that is. It saves me the trouble of trying to explain to them where Pompano is located, only to have them tell me they don't know where that is. It's as if my hometown isn't on any maps, so people don't realize it exists unless they are from that area.

I always get excited when someone tells me they're from the area. Then, the conversation lights up because I feel like we have a connection. It feels good to have a connection with people; to know you have something in common with them. Commonality makes life so much easier.

I am the middle child between two sisters. An interesting fact about me is that my older sister and I share the same birthdate: May 3rd. We are exactly one year apart. When my sister was having her 1st birthday party, mama was at the hospital giving birth to me. I always wondered how that happened. I don't know if I was born early, late, or on the original due date, but God wanted me to come on that day.

I will forever share that special day with my sister. That, among other things, is something that made me feel so connected to her throughout my childhood. She's been my best friend from birth; we have always been super close. Although there were times when life happened and we were at odds with each other, we will **always** have a special connection. We've endured so many hard things together, so there will forever be a unique bond between us.

My parents were young when they gave birth to me; mama was 18, and daddy was 20. Since they were so young, they didn't know much about parenting. Despite their age, my parents did the best they could with what they had. The thing about parenting is that we all do the best we can with our knowledge and skills. We pray and read books but sometimes, we still get things wrong. We learn as we go! My parents had a hard life together. They loved each other but raising their little family had a lot of challenges.

Anytime we face uphill battles in life, we sometimes seek help from those around us. I grew up around a lot of family members, so there was always someone willing to lend a hand.

No matter how old you are when your first baby comes along, it's never easy. I remember when I gave birth to my son, I was so nervous. I didn't want to make any mistakes. I wanted his life to be perfect. No matter who you are, being a new parent is always scary and a work in progress. Yes, there are plenty of people to give advice and share their experiences with you, but you're the one who is responsible for this new life.

I remember the story of how my Godmother became an integral part of my life. She would tell me this story about as many times as I asked to hear it. When she told the story, you could see in her eyes that it was a joyous moment for her. It was as if it were one of the happiest days of her life!

My family worshipped at a little church in the neighborhood called Hopewell Baptist Church. The church wasn't very big. Once you walked through the door, you could see everything from the back door to the choir loft. My grandmother, aunts, uncles, and other family members all attended this church.

It was a Sunday, shortly after my mother had given birth to me. Everyone wanted to see the new baby, so they crowded around to peek. My Godmother told me she fell in love as soon as she saw me in my mother's arms. At that moment, she wanted to be a part of my life. I'm not sure if she ever realized that was part of God's ultimate plan for both my life and hers. After looking at the new bundle of joy, she jokingly asked if she could take me home with her one day. To her delight, my mom said, **"Yes!"** That was the beginning of something beautiful.

As a new mother, I remember being so attached to my babies. I couldn't bear to have them out of my sight for a moment. I was always paranoid that something would happen if they weren't with me. Some would say I was a *little* obsessive. As such, the fact that my mother so easily allowed my Godmother to play such a huge role in my life is very telling…

When I think about it, I know that it was a God-moment for my mother and Godmother. Jeremiah 29:11 says, *"For I know the plans I have for you, says the Lord, they are plans for good and not for disaster, to give you a future and a hope."* God **knew** who I would need in my life to be the woman I am today. There are so many aspects about my beginning that have intrigued me for many years. The way that God orchestrated every direction my life has taken amazes me. He placed my Godmother in the right place and had her ask the right question. I believe she was being led by Him to secure a place in my life.

I used to struggle with this until I realized the **magnitude** of my mother's response to the question she was asked that day. There was a time when I was unable to care for my son—my firstborn child—during my service in the U.S. Army. He lived with my mother for about six months. At the time, I was stationed at Fort Bragg, North Carolina. There were over 600 miles between my new baby and me. The decision was not an easy one for me to make, but I knew it was best for my child.

As mothers, we put our children first and make decisions that are often right for them and not us. My mother must've known her decision to allow this woman of God to share in the responsibility of raising me was the right one. It proved to be one of the greatest decisions she made for my life. Even though it was a decision that was best for her child, I can only imagine how it must've affected her.

During the time my son was with my mama, I struggled with feeling like a bad mother. In retrospect, I realize that a good mother is one who sometimes makes hard decisions that prove to be exactly what their children need at the time. Whenever I was with my Godmother, my mom knew I was safe and in good hands. She had the security of knowing that I was well provided for and that I was with someone who had my best interests in mind as much as she did. She also knew my Godmother would always take great care of me. The main thing that must've calmed her was the knowledge that my Godmother loved me as much as she did. She loved me like her own. She not only poured love into me; my Godmother also planted the Word of God in my heart. That's where my foundation began. Whenever I was with her, she'd spend hours talking to me about the Word of God.

I remember **hating** to learn the Books of the Bible or memorize scripture. God knew what I needed because of the path ahead. He was preparing me to be able to face anything. That's what He does! He makes sure we're equipped with what we need, even before we know we'll need it.

The day came when I lost my Godmother, but I will **never** forget the value of what she gave me and the huge part she played in me being the strong woman of God I am today. Without the things she instilled in me, I would've never been able to face what was to come.

The Games We Played

Many children grow up with fond memories of their childhood. They can recall happy times they shared or fun things they did. I often joke with my husband that he had a "gravy train" childhood—one that was filled with all the love a child could want. He has fond memories of family gatherings and thoughts of the affectionate way he was cared for by the people in his life.

He lived in a loving environment where he never had to question if he was wanted. He never questioned his being. Although his birth wasn't planned, his mother loved him unconditionally and treated him like the gift he is. In contrast, my childhood was unlike his. I have a few glimpses of happy moments growing up but, for the most part, it wasn't a childhood I would wish on anyone.

I grew up feeling like I was a bother; like I was always in the way. I didn't feel like I was worthy of anything good in life. I allowed people to treat me with little regard because I felt it was what I deserved. Who would want me now that I had nothing to offer? Who would want me once they knew I had been touched? I was no longer pure! The best parts of me had been taken…stolen.

I was not like the other little girls who had been saved from being violated. They possessed something I had lost long ago. My innocence was no longer mine. It was ripped away from me! I could no longer offer purity to my future husband because it wasn't mine to give due to someone else's greed snatching it out of my grasp. I was left with only pieces of who I was supposed to be. I didn't want to go into the world as an imposter, so I wore the clothing of a girl who had been used and abused. That is the identity I chose because it was who I was now.

I have vivid memories of the first time he touched me. I was five years old, and he was one of the people who was trusted by my parents. They expected him to love me…**and that's just what he did.** Unbeknownst to them, his version of "love" was distorted. Since he had my parents' trust, he also had mine. I looked up to him as a child should look at her uncle.

Before that time, he was one of my favorite people to spend time with. He was fun and played fun games with my sister and me. Some games, he made up himself. He wasn't stuffy like most of the other adults in my life. Growing up, we were never allowed to be around adults, especially when they were talking. We always had to be outside playing. If it was light outside, then that's where we were supposed to stay until just before dark. My uncle was different, though. We always knew he enjoyed having us around. We were a joy to him!

He used to make these amazing peanut butter and jelly sandwiches for us. They weren't the kind you think of with the peanut butter on one slice of bread and jelly on the other. No. His were "special sandwiches." He would mix the peanut butter and jelly, and **then** spread it on the bread. It tasted heavenly! That was a ritual he did every time we saw him. It was also one of the reasons we saw him as the "cool uncle."

One of the games we played was called "The Devil with a Pitchfork."

> *"Devil with the pitchfork, what do you want?*
> *A color! What color?"*

At that point, he would choose a color. If it was the one you had chosen, he would then chase you around the room until he caught you. The game and rules were like that of "Duck, Duck, Goose."

I know it's a strange name for a game. I didn't realize it then because little girls don't question adults in their life, but the name of the game was symbolic of his evil intentions. The game was his way of making little girls feel safe. He made what he was going to do to us seem "fun." It was a distraction from the pain he would cause in our lives then and years into our future.

If it's fun, it must be okay to do. Since he was the only one who played games with us, if we told, the fun would stop. This game represented light versus darkness. He was the darkness that took us from our world filled with baby dolls and castles to one of thorns and thistles. The wicked witch really did exist, and so did the dragons.

The game represented so many things that weren't good. It was the difference between good and evil. There was a dividing line, and once he crossed it, we couldn't go back to the children we once were. We could no longer be little girls dreaming about magical things. Instead, once he deflowered us, we had to deal with adult things. No longer were our dreams filled with fairytales. We used to daydream about all the things that would happen when we were introduced to our knight in shining armor. The one thing we don't think about is the wedding night because our young minds only dreamt of magical things.

Now, we were exposed to this new world—a world filled with **sex** and **secrets**. This world wasn't a cheerful one. It wasn't filled with the laughter of little girls with no worries. Instead, there were lots of tears and pain.

It all started so innocently. He used to play games with us when he visited after school each day. He'd play with us while we waited for our parents to come home from work. We looked forward to playing because whenever he was there, he never made us do our homework. We looked forward to coming home every day, so much so that we'd **RUN** home from the bus stop.

Then, one day, everything changed. It wasn't fun anymore. I often wonder if it was his plan all along. How long did he take to gain our full trust? Did he know we would be easy targets? Or was there any fear of us telling our parents what he was doing to their children? I also wonder if my sister and I were the only ones whose lives he destroyed with his perversion. I wonder what it was inside him that caused him to want to do those horrible acts. Was he struggling with inner demons? How could he hurt little girls who adored him? He used to be one of my favorite people—until he removed the blinders from my eyes. Instead of seeing my loving uncle, I only saw the monster he had become to me. Did he genuinely love us? I've always had so many questions that I'll never have the chance to ask him. His despicable actions not only changed the way we viewed him but now we saw the world through ugly lenses.

We may never understand all the reasons why things happen to us, but God says He will work **ALL** things together for our good. I believe that even this situation has worked for my good. For many years, I felt like I needed to know why. Why did he do that to me? There was a time I wanted to have a conversation with someone like him. I needed to understand what goes on in the mind of a child molester. Even if it wouldn't bring closure for me, my finite mind always needed to know that there was a reason why. It's as if knowing why would've made what he did easier to deal with.

Children gain their identity in the first five years of their life. Things like who they will become, what their personality will be, and how they think of themselves are all formed during this period. For the most part, I was a happy child until that time. Then, my world was altered. No more sunshine and pretty flowers. There were only cloudy skies.

I had experiences I didn't understand. Was it normal? Was it what we were supposed to be doing? Children should never be placed in the position of understanding adult things. As adults, we should be able to reflect on our childhood with beautiful memories, not horrifying tales of acts done to us.

Children are blessings from God to be loved and enjoyed. They are **not** objects to be used to fulfill selfish desires. In my young mind, I couldn't distinguish right from wrong. I just knew I didn't like what was happening to me. I wondered why it was a secret we had to keep from everyone. We couldn't tell our parents about the game that was only played when no one else was around.

I don't think my sister or I had the thought to tell our parents what was going on. We didn't even talk about it with each other. It's like we pretended that part of our lives didn't exist. My daddy was very close to his family, and he loved his brother. Would he believe us if we told? Would he think we were making it all up? Would it cause problems in the family? I love my daddy, and I didn't want to tell him something so horrible. I just wanted things to go back to how they used to be. It would've been so much easier.

I'm writing from my childhood memories, and I can only write what I remember. I don't recall ever having the urge to tell. During that time, I remember I started sleepwalking and wetting the bed. I vividly remember one of these occasions. One night, I had gotten out of bed while sleepwalking. My mom found me in our room closet the next morning. To her dismay, I had wet myself. This scenario occurred regularly. During the times I spent weekends with my Godmother, she would double-bolt the doors to ensure I didn't leave the house while sleepwalking.

I know that children sleepwalk and/or wet the bed. Most often, it's a normal part of childhood. I've also heard people say that bed-wetting and sleepwalking are both signs that a child is being sexually abused. I wonder if my parents saw those signs as an indication that something was wrong with their baby girl. I don't remember if my sister experienced any of the same things.

As a parent, you don't expect awful things to happen to your babies. You hear about it happening to others, but rarely anyone you know. Well, at least not that anyone openly shares with you. Molestation affects other families, not yours. It's easy to pretend it happens in other people's worlds.

Today, I see many campaigns that talk to children about "safe touch." I don't remember anything like that when I was growing up. In the 70s, things like sexual abuse in the family wasn't a subject that was discussed. It was kept as a family secret because there was so much shame surrounding it. The subject was taboo! Even when we finally told my dad, I don't recall it ever being talked about after that.

I don't know if that is what caused the distance and turmoil between my parents or if it was why they decided to seek a divorce. I can only guess it must've been difficult for both of my parents to know their little girls had been violated by someone they knew, loved, and trusted.

Now that I'm older, I understand molestation to be a sickness. More than a few little boys and girls are affected. *"About one in 10 children will be sexually abused before their 18th birthday. About one in seven girls and one in 25 boys will be sexually abused before they turn 18"* (Townsend & Rheingold, 2013).

If you say you were sexually abused as a child, it's like, *"Join the club! So was I!"* Unfortunately, this isn't a club **anyone** would ever *willingly* volunteer to join.

The Divorce

Most children are horrified when they find out their parents are getting a divorce. I can't recall what my exact feelings were at the time, but I do remember I missed having my dad around. I didn't see him as much anymore and eventually, he moved to another city. Although we spent some holidays and summers with him, it wasn't the same as having him at home with us.

The one thing I do recall being happy about was the lack of fighting between my parents. Both my mom and dad were the best parents they knew how to be, but it was their relationship with each other that was a problem. I knew they both loved my sisters and me very much and wanted to provide a good home for us. As a child, it's hard to understand why two people who are individually amazing to you can't be the same way with each other.

Children need and deserve to grow up in an environment that allows them to thrive. It's like planting flowers. You must make the right choices for the flowers to grow and thrive. The things you must consider are:

- The right season to plant
- The proper soil in which to plant them
- Food
- Adequate sunlight

If **any** of those elements are off in **any** way, the flowers may not grow properly. When you choose a place to plant them, the soil should be good, or you must purchase the proper fertilizers. Then, there needs to be a proper balance of sunlight mixed with the correct plant food. If you plant the flowers in the wrong season, they'll die or not grow as they should.

That illustration is not meant to make raising children sound as menial as growing flowers; however, I'm trying to make a correlation to what's important in a child's life for them to grow to be healthy adults. The basic needs of a child are food, clothing, and shelter. They also need to be loved and nurtured or they won't be who they were created to be. A child also needs to know they are in a safe place.

Strangely enough, it's sometimes better for children to grow up in a single-parent home rather than one where two parents argue and fight all the time. Yes, being in a single-parent home is not optimal, but it is much better than growing up in a dysfunctional one. That is one of the realizations that wasn't easy for me to come to when I was raising my own children. At the time, I felt that no matter what, children needed both parents in the home. That was a thought I later found to be incorrect.

Once my dad moved away, so many things changed. He eventually remarried and went on with his life. During our visits with him, everything was different because he had someone new in his life. It was weird for us seeing him with someone other than our mother. The transition wasn't as easy as it could have been for us, my dad, and his new wife. He was in love, and we just felt like we were in the way. We wanted him all to ourselves without someone else being there. That's how it is with children; they just want to know where they fit in. We didn't feel like we had a place in my dad's new life anymore. It seemed like he was so much happier with his new wife than he had been with us. We knew he still loved us, but it just wasn't the same.

As a result, my mom became a single mother of three girls. Since our extended family surrounded us, there were always people around to help her with caring for us. Things changed in her financial status, and she worked harder than before because she was the sole provider, but we were good. Oftentimes, we think we need all the "bells and whistles," but all we really need is love. There were things we had to do without, but again, our home was a peaceful one.

I remember so many days when my sisters and I would stay outside for hours, catching and playing with grasshoppers, climbing trees, and just having fun in the sun. Those were simple times—ones that many children today will never experience. It seems that life was simpler then—compared to how things are today.

For a long time, we were good. It was just my mom and us girls. Then, the day came when everything changed. My mom met someone! Change can sometimes be good. It can represent something you haven't experienced before. It represents a new beginning. The change brought a smile to my mom's face. She was different. She seemed happy about having a new man in her life.

He appeared to be an "okay" person. Of course, that was the opinion of an 11-year-old. What did I know? When we are looking at things from a child's perspective, we can't quite comprehend things we feel about someone. We may feel something, but we don't understand it enough to put it into words others can comprehend. We just know we either like them or we don't. If they are mean to us, then instantly, we don't like them. If they are nice to us the first time we meet, then we immediately think we like them. Then, there are the times when you get a shiver up your spine when you're around them, but you think it must be because you're cold. One day, you'll think back to that moment and realize: It wasn't the cold.

I remember when my baby girl first met the father of my three older children. She cried whenever she was near him. Although he tried, there was nothing he could do to win her over. I didn't understand why she just wouldn't warm up to him until years later when I realized there was something about him she just didn't like. It was as if she could see through all his fluff and charm straight to his soul. She could see who he really was, even though he was good at hiding it from the rest of us. When she looked at him, she saw the wolf in the sheep's clothing when everyone else just saw the sheep.

Children have an intuition about people that we, as adults, reason away. We ignore those gut feelings. Jesus said we are to come to Him as little children. Children have the purest hearts and see things that we shrug away. Maybe — just maybe — we should listen to them more often.

My first impression of my mom's new mate was that he made my mother happy and her life easier. I had already seen what the divorce did to my mother and how sad it made her, so I wasn't going to "make any waves" to mess this new thing up for her. The life of a single mother is never an easy one. There are so many demands on you, with all of them holding equal importance. It often feels like you're drinking out of a fire hose trying to get water. When I was a single mother, it always seemed like I could never catch my breath. There was always just one more thing that needed my attention. Once I put one fire out, there were five more raging and waiting for me.

When my current husband came along, he was a breath of fresh air! Not only did he make my life easier, but he made life more bearable. I had someone to share all my burdens. Life wasn't as hard as it had been when it was only me. As a single parent, sometimes we're so tired, we miss the warning signs when someone new comes into our life. They say and do all the right things and you think, *"Maybe this is a gift from God! Maybe he's an answer to the prayers I've been sending up every night!"* I wonder if that was how my mother felt when she met her new man…

My previous pastor once said to me, *"There are two types of people: the ones who pray for you and those who prey on you."* I believe that man was the latter. He saw what he wanted and started his grooming from the very beginning. I'm not so naïve to think he didn't have a plan when he encountered my mother and her three beautiful, little girls. No. He had an ulterior motive for offering her the world. He wanted something in return that would serve his selfish and evil desires. It was a strategy that he must've known to use when he saw her.

By the time anyone figured out his strategy, it was too late. The damage had already been done. There was no way to turn back and rethink decisions made; no way to take back what had been stolen. Why did these things keep happening to us? It's as if there was a bull's eye on our backs that only the vilest of human beings could see.

Here we go again… The prey is in the trap!

Tyria D. Jones

Here We Go Again

Shortly after the beginning of our mother's new relationship, our life began to change **very** quickly. It seemed it was for the better. Not only was this new man showering our mother with nice things, but he was also spoiling her girls. Life was getting easier, and we'd soon have more of the things we missed out on after the divorce.

We lived in the housing projects for a while after my parents divorced, but it was nice because we were surrounded by our cousins. My grandmother lived down the street from us, so we could visit her anytime we wanted to do so. Living in the same neighborhood as everyone we knew was nice and made growing up much more fun.

When we moved to Fort Lauderdale with my mom's new man, it was not a happy time. Yes, we were in a nice house, but we were away from all our family and friends. Before the move, not only had we been able to walk to school every morning, we also lived in the same neighborhood as most of the people we went to school with. After the move, we were in an unfamiliar place. A new living situation wasn't the only change we had to adjust to. There were more changes to come that would be more complicated, to say the least.

It was difficult getting used to all the changes because they happened so quickly. We had to adjust to a man being in the house with us, especially after having our mom to ourselves for so long. We wanted her to be happy, just not with someone other than our daddy. What started as a happy time quickly turned into something we began to hate. My mom's life was easier, but our lives became increasingly harder with each new day.

This new man seemed to want to do *everything* to ensure we had the things we needed — and even a lot of the things us little girls wanted. As little girls, we loved playing make-believe. Unfortunately, our new life was no fairytale. What started as the perfect transition from a broken home to one that had two "parents" would end up being something that was better left undone.

After the divorce from my first husband, it took me a **long time** to start dating again. I didn't want someone pretending to love me while, at the same time, preying on my children. It's so hard for women with children to remarry because of all the dangers it presents to our children. We pray for a good man, but we don't always know what's underneath the surface of his charm. My children had already experienced the horror inflicted on them by their biological father. How could I trust that some unknown man would be good to both my children and me as well?

Once we become mothers, things aren't about us anymore; they are about the little blessings God has entrusted us with. They aren't "miniature adults" (as I've often heard them referred to as), so they aren't supposed to be able to handle things that even we, as adults, struggle with. Children are open slates of innocence waiting to be poured into. We must pour the right things into them to ensure they become everything they were brought into this world to be.

During my childhood years, there were so many times I wished I could be older. I didn't want to be a child anymore. It was too hard. That isn't something new because children say, *"I can't wait to be 'this age' or 'that age' so I can do what I want to do,"* all the time. The difference is that my wishing wasn't for reasons such as that. Instead, I wanted to be older so that I could have a voice. It seemed like the adults around me—the ones who were supposed to protect me—had other priorities than ensuring my safety. We went from one bad situation to another, and it seemed like it was a never-ending thing.

I used to say that parenting is hard because children don't come with a handbook. We don't get instructions for how to properly raise them. That, however, is an erroneous statement. We *DO* have a handbook given to us by God: **The Holy Bible.** If we follow it and the principles outlined within, yes, we will still make mistakes, but overall, we'll have a straightforward guide to follow.

Life with this new man started to look like a scene in a movie we'd been in before, except the roles were a little different. We had all the physical things we could ever want…if we each played the role we were given. Being a child was difficult when it shouldn't have been. Children shouldn't be afraid to go to sleep at night. They shouldn't fear the boogie man. Yes, I know that all children believe in scary things they see on television. The difference with us was that our boogie man wasn't on television; he was the man who lived with us. He was this new man who said he loved us. He was the man in the next room.

It all started so innocently one year. We were going to do something different for Christmas that year. Instead of him and mom buying all of us presents to put under the tree, we'd all exchange names and buy gifts for the person whose name we chose. It seemed like an excellent idea when he suggested it. It would be a way for each of us to participate, and it would be less expensive for them. Of course, they were the ones giving us the money for the presents, so I guess that part wasn't so important.

We all chose our names, and he pulled mine. At the time, I remember being happy because that meant I'd get a good gift. In my childlike excitement, I had no way of knowing that wasn't such a good thing for me. I had no way of knowing what it would turn into. I also had no way of knowing that was part of his plan…and the beginning stages of him grooming me.

I'm sure he saw the vulnerabilities in my sisters and me. We had "daddy issues"! By the time he came along, we were seeing our daddy less frequently. The visits didn't happen as often as we'd like, so we were all looking for and needing that male role model. We needed someone to validate us because we were feeling unwanted due to all the changes. I don't know if he knew we'd "been there, done that" already. We'd been in that place between being a child and being exposed to adult things. Did he know someone else had already violated me? Is that why I was chosen? Was I an easy target?

It's so hard to comprehend what goes through the mind of a man when he can look at a child and see a sexual being.

That Christmas was the start of an ugly relationship between he and I. I used the word "relationship" very loosely. The more accurate way to describe it is him raping me every opportunity he got. I didn't understand why I was put in this place called **HELL** again. Why couldn't I be like other little girls? Instead, I was violently pushed into adulthood every time he touched me.

We try to protect our children from the things we see or the things we think they may face, but what about the people we allow into their lives? I remember sitting in assemblies at school where police officers would talk to us about "Stranger Danger." They'd tell us not to get into a car with strangers or even talk to someone we didn't know. *If only I could have told them the danger was in my home...* I couldn't let them know that the person hurting me was not a stranger, but someone who was supposed to love and protect me.

I remember our mom being adamant about us walking home from school together. We'd get into a lot of trouble if we didn't arrive home with each other. So many people were trying to keep us safe from the hands of strangers instead of looking behind closed doors for the real danger.

The sexual assault went on for years. It became a part of life for me and something I came to expect. When you've lived with the abuse for so long, it becomes your new normal. It's just what you do. I was no longer a little girl; I was a woman in a little girl's body. I could no longer identify with girls my age because I had other thoughts running through my head. **Would it ever end?**

Secrets

The question that is sometimes asked of children who are abused is: **WHY?** Why not tell someone you trust? Why not tell a teacher or a trusted adult? There must be SOMEONE in your life you trust enough to expose those dark secrets!

Sometimes, it's not about having someone you can trust. There are so many reasons why a child may choose not to disclose their truths. Will they be believed? Maybe the adult will think they're making it all up. What if they do believe the child? Will they be the one to come to their rescue, or will they act as if it didn't happen? Maybe it'll be better for the family if no one says anything.

The one thing children want to know above anything else is that their parents will keep them **safe**. They want to know that no matter what, they are important. They want to know that should someone try to harm them, their parents will come to their rescue. These are things all children have the right to expect, but it doesn't always happen that way.

When my uncle was the perpetrator, I did tell—but nothing was done! We just moved forward and pretended it didn't happen. Maybe it was easier for the adults to go on and not address it for the sake of keeping the peace in the family. I remember feeling so betrayed. Why didn't someone—the people who should've done so—fight for me? I remember our visits to my grandmother's house stopped once that secret was revealed. Maybe they felt that was enough. Maybe they thought that was the best way to deal with the situation.

I was no longer the little girl who believed her daddy would save her from the dragons. I had no confidence that he would be the one to slay the big, bad wolf. When my mother's new friend violated me, I didn't feel that I could go to my father for help; nor did I think my mother could handle what I had to say about the man who had saved her from so much struggle. I was on my own and dealt with it the best way I knew how…in silence. There would be no one to come to my aid. I had to be my own protector.

Children who are forced to deal with adult things develop a tough outer shell. They learn to hide what they are feeling deep down inside. They become self-reliant and present a strong exterior to the world. I was the child who never wanted anyone to see my weaknesses. I didn't want anyone to see how vulnerable I truly was. If they did, maybe they'd be the next one to thrust me into their dark world. I had no escape from the place that man had taken me.

He trained me to know what my role was, so I accepted it. It was the same drill every night. Once my mom and sisters were asleep, I knew he'd be coming for me soon after. There was always one undeniable signal that left no doubt in my mind what was about to happen: As I listened to the shower, I dreaded hearing the end to that sound. I didn't want him to repeat what he did night after night. *Maybe he'd spare me…*

I laid in bed praying **every** night that this would be the night he chose to go to sleep next to my mother, instead of coming to my room. Most nights, my prayers went unanswered. Once the shower stopped, I knew he'd be headed my way…naked. There was no denying what was to come next.

The one thing no one talks about is how sexual abuse affects a little girl before she is ready for womanhood. What does it do to her body, her emotions, and her mind? Those were the three things battling for my attention each day. My body betrayed me each time it responded to the animal who chose to see me as his sexual toy. Although I had the mind of a child, my body responded to him like that of a woman. I hated myself! How could there be a physical response to the actions of a monster? It was all so confusing and left me feeling guilty. Was it my fault? Had I sent signals of some type to him? My body was reacting to something that was happening, and I had no control over any of it.

The abuse occurred for some time leading up to my teenage years. I was old enough to know what it was. I was also old enough to understand it was wrong. Why did I feel so guilty about something I had no control over? I didn't want to hurt my mother. I didn't want her to hate me. Would she think I led him on? Would she believe me? I had already lost my daddy to someone else. I couldn't take a chance and lose my mother, too. I had no one!

Although I prayed for it to stop, it was hard to believe there was a God who looked down on me and allowed that horrible thing to happen time and again. What was wrong with me that He sent **NO ONE** to help? Was I expendable? Maybe God didn't hear my prayers. *That had to be it.* Otherwise, it would've been like Him leaving 'Little Red Riding Hood' in the hands of the big, bad wolf. If God didn't' hear my prayers or my cries at night, there was no one to save me. Who else could I have gone to? I didn't want to burden my dad and mom again. I didn't want to put that in their lap because it would mess things up for everyone.

The adults around me had made me painfully aware of how unimportant I was to them. I wasn't worth saving. I wasn't worth the turmoil that would come from holding others accountable for their actions. I was surrounded by people yet felt all alone. I felt abandoned, like someone had dropped me and refused to pick me up. I often wonder if they saw the signs. Did they see how much I was struggling? Did they notice the light go out in my eyes? If so, what did they attribute it to?

Some people say that not all children show signs of abuse, but, in my opinion, I can't say that I agree. I know that my sister and I both exhibited signs that something was going on with us. We displayed them in different ways, but the signs were definitely there. All it took was for those around us to pay attention. It's difficult raising children and protecting them from every conceivable thing that could be of harm to them. We can write a list of the many dangers our children could encounter, but it would be impossible to know every danger around every corner.

When I was younger (and before having children), I had many issues with my parents because I felt like they abandoned me. I carried bitterness toward both for all the things and people they failed to protect me from. After I became a parent and carried the responsibility of protecting my own children, I realized how unfair I had been toward my own parents. There is no way we can always cover our children. Yes, we pray for them daily, but only God can completely protect them from **ALL** the things that could happen to them. When we are blessed to be parents, we must know that with the blessing also comes a burden—one we carry the rest of our lives. We will always be a parent, but we can't always be there at every moment to shield them.

When we're brought into this world, God already knows the things we will be faced with. He sees our beginning and our ending, so He knows the good things and the bad things we will come up against. As parents, the best thing we can do for our children is to raise them in a way that they have a relationship with God. It is what will help them through every rough patch they encounter along life's journey. That relationship will give them the strength to keep going when they face situations like what I experienced as a child.

I couldn't bring myself to tell anyone about the horror I was experiencing, but God had a ram in the bush. Even when we feel like He's forgotten us or isn't there as we go through difficult times, the fact is that He **IS** there.

"I will never leave you nor forsake you."
Hebrews 13:5

During the times I laid in bed dreading the horrible events that would happen to me night after night, God had a plan to deliver me. I had no idea about the relief that He was sending. Relief, yes…and it would come sooner than I thought. My prayers **were** being answered!

The Revelation

It was such a relief for all of it to finally be out in the open. We would finally get him to stop. There would be no more nights of me lying awake, waiting for him to come into my room. I'd no longer have to dread the sky getting dark because I knew what came with the darkness. We'd be free again! But free to do what? We couldn't say we could go back to being children. That part of us was gone forever. Not one, but **TWO** thieves stole that from us.

Once that part of yourself has been opened, your body can't go back to the way it used to be before a man touched you. It's like a door was opened and something is preventing it from ever closing again. In the spiritual sense, now we will fight things that our young souls were never prepared for. Physically, our bodies will yearn for his touch, yet our minds will feel like we're betraying ourselves. How can we desire such ugliness?

It's our fault because we should've known better. We should've seen it coming. We'd already been through it, so the signs should've been like neon lights flashing before our eyes. The thing about being molested is that it never happens quickly. It's a subtle attack. It happens, and then you're left wondering how you didn't see it coming. He was as subtle as the snake in the Garden of Eden. His approach was one I'm sure he'd practiced on others and continued to do so until he had it perfected.

I wonder if any of his other victims had seen their assault coming or if they were taken by surprise, too? Yes, there were others before us—and probably others after us. The sad thing about molestation is that it's an ugliness that no one likes to talk about. Everyone wants to pretend it doesn't happen, so that leaves too much room for many children to be subjected to it. Most perpetrators get away with it and are never held accountable for the vile acts against children. They are free to move from victim to victim. Well, he was no different. **He was never held accountable.**

The only ones who are punished are the innocent souls who must live with the horrible memories. Some are even told that it never happened. They are then victimized again by those who are supposed to be their protectors. This time, the assault is like a knife wound to the heart because they are made to feel like they are just trying to get attention or telling lies for no reason. A child rarely says something so ugly if it's not true.

I don't know why my mother believed the abuse was happening, but she did. It may have been because neither my older sister nor I were the ones to tell her; it was our little sister. I really can't tell you how she knew about the abuse. I don't even know where she got the courage to tell, but I can say she was my rescuer that day. My little sister is three years younger than me, so the fact that she was brave enough to expose the secret amazes me. That was the day she became my hero.

Although my younger sister hadn't been touched, the abuse scarred her as much as it did my older sister and me. She had to carry the heavy burden—one that shouldn't have been on the mind of a child her age. I often wonder how many nights she laid awake, knowing what was happening to her older sisters? How did all of that make her feel? We never discussed any of it after that time. Again, our family just glossed over that period in our lives. It was a trauma none of us cared to revisit.

Even when it's not discussed, a situation such as the one we were all dealing with continues to cut like a double-edged sword. No one is safe from the wounds it causes. We were all trying to recover from our injuries, so we couldn't help each other heal. As I recall these memories, it's as if I'm talking about someone else's life and I'm reading it in disbelief. We were all babies, yet we were forced to live in a war zone.

The funny thing about everything that happened is that we all thought once the secrets were exposed, our lives would change instantly. We wouldn't be subjected to having no room door or being told to leave the bathroom door open as we took our bath nightly. We thought he'd no longer be able to rub us down with baby oil after we showered and, most importantly, he wouldn't be able to choose between my sister and me like we were "the flavor of the day."

We confirmed what my sister told our mother, she believed it, and now we'd move out of his house, right? **WRONG!** Unfortunately, that's not at all how it went.

We were living in a nightmare. Everything went from **bad** to *worse*. As a child, it's hard to understand how things work. All children think is that one plus one equals two. Sadly, things aren't always that simple.

Although our mother worked outside the home, her job didn't provide enough for her to support us on her own. The perpetrator had set a trap and made her dependent on him. Why didn't she just take us and leave? Wouldn't it have been better to be homeless than under the same roof with the man who raped your daughters? Everyone can look at a situation and say what they would've done had it been them, but no one ever knows what they'd **REALLY** do until they're confronted with the harsh reality.

I can say what I **WISH** she would've done, but I can't speak for our mother. The older I got, the more I understood the pressures of making the best decision for my own children. No matter what decision we make, it can always be second-guessed by others at any moment. There are choices I made as a mother that I can look back at now and say they were the wrong ones, but it's because I'm no longer in the heat of the situation. Stress, along with the feelings of hopelessness and helplessness, can cause us to have compromised judgment.

It was *months* before we were able to escape his grasp, and it was even longer before we were **completely** out of his reach. When someone like him plants their claws into you, it takes years before you're able to close all the piercing holes left behind. Although we were able to break free, the turmoil of our lives was far from over. Sometimes, you think things are better if you can just escape the current hell you're in. The thing you may not realize is that there is something that may be worse than that…

I was in high school by this time and had lived most of my life being the object of someone else's tormenting. I longed for the day when I could make my own decisions. I wanted so much to be able to have a voice, to speak for myself. I guess these are all the reasons I gravitated toward unhealthy relationships. I hated who I was because of everything I had been through. Up to this point, life had shown me that others could take from me whatever they pleased and leave once the damage was done.

I was broken!

I was defeated!

I felt like nothing!

I longed for someone to love me!

I was an accident waiting to happen!

The day came when it was time for me to leave the misery of my life at home. I had an escape route, even if it meant marrying the wrong man for all the wrong reasons. We sometimes make decisions out of desperation. We want an escape, so we turn to whatever will numb that pain. Marrying the wrong man was my "drug of choice." It would be one bad decision after another until the day I was tired of looking for love in all the wrong places — the day I turned to my Heavenly Father to fill the void I had in my heart. That was the day I found true, unconditional love.

Tyria D. Jones

Never Enough

Have you ever felt that you just can't do **anything** right or like you are constantly trying to measure up to someone else's standard, but never quite making it? That was me for most of my life. I've often felt like I didn't measure up to some invisible standard. If I was in a room full of other girls, I always felt like I wasn't as pretty as any of them. No matter how many times someone told me I was pretty, it didn't matter. I didn't believe them. I always saw something different when I looked in the mirror. It was the same with not feeling like I was smart enough. Although I graduated in the top of my class, I wasn't number one, so it wasn't good enough. If I wasn't the best or at the very top, then it wasn't enough. I could've been better!

I've always held myself to an impossible standard. I remember when one of my daughters would come home with an 'A' on a test. If she didn't receive a 100% on it, I'd always ask her, *"Why?"* Or I'd say, *"Couldn't you have gotten an 'A+' instead of an 'A'?"* Of course, she knew I wasn't being serious with her, and we'd laugh about it. She's always been very smart and never made poor grades. I had confidence that she always did her best. The thing about this example is that this is how hard I've always been on myself. I had to be the best and, when I wasn't, I considered myself a failure.

There was an inner voice that always told me I would never and could never measure up. I sometimes wondered why I even tried. No matter what that voice said, I still tried to shut it out and prove myself wrong. Where did that voice come from? Why was it always so loud in my head? I didn't understand why I had this unbearable need to do everything right. The voice was with me constantly.

The problem with these inner voices is if they aren't saying the things God says or would say to you, they can be dangerous. They can cause you to measure yourself by the wrong things or people. If you listen to those voices too long, you'll begin to see yourself as a failure in everything. If someone says you're not good enough in one area, you'll attribute that statement to not just that area, but your whole life.

I've made so many mistakes in my life. Sometimes, the weight of those bad decisions takes me down a long road that leads to the pit of despair. Then, I begin to think about how my life would've been had I done something different. That only leads to regrets and wishing I could go back and change things in my past.

"Finally, brethren, whatsoever things are true, whatsoever things are honest, whatsoever things are just, whatsoever things are pure, whatsoever things are lovely, whatsoever things are of good report, if there be any virtue, and if there be any praise, think on these things."
Philippians 4:8

We ought to think good things about ourselves, instead of what the enemy desires us to think. The truth is that no matter what anyone says about us or to us, we will always be our own worst critic. We don't need help from anyone else or a lesson showing us how to beat ourselves up. It comes naturally engrained in us.

I believe God knew in our human weakness that our thoughts would lead us into places He never meant for us to go. Wherever your thoughts are, that's where your actions will tend to go. If you think a certain way long enough, you begin to believe it. You'll convince yourself that those thoughts in your head are correct and start to agree with them. The Bible tells us that whatever a man thinks, so is he (Proverbs 23:7). The many years I've thought of myself as a failure, I became a failure in my own eyes.

When you think you can't do anything, there's no way you will ever accomplish the things that you were put on this Earth to do. Before we came to this world through our mothers, God assigned a purpose to each of us. Your purpose is not the same as mine. We each are given an assignment that no one else in the world in this time, times past, or in the future can fulfill. There have been billions of people who have lived and will live on this Earth, but none of us have the exact same purpose. Think about that for a moment…

There are people who only I can reach. If I walk through this life wasting time thinking about how much of a failure I am instead of focusing on the purpose God gave me, then those people will not get what they need to fulfill their purpose. Yes, I believe God can direct them to someone else, but the original assignment is mine, not theirs.

So, why did I see myself as a failure? It all goes back to my beginning. I failed to keep the hands of my first molester off me. Yes, I was only five years old when it happened. I was a helpless child. Why, then, did I blame myself for something I couldn't have possibly stopped? The mind is not always rational, and our thoughts don't always make sense. Even at that young age, I began to blame myself and felt responsible for my own torture. Why didn't I say something? Why didn't I do something? I could've or should've told him no or made him stop.

The thing our young minds don't realize is that we didn't have a voice because it was taken from us. It wasn't in our power to override a decision that had already been made for us.

Then, to be abused repeatedly in some form throughout my life meant it must be me, right? No, that's **NOT** right. However, when you've been victimized more than once by different people, you begin to see yourself as a common factor. The problem isn't them; it's you! That's what you have told yourself every time it happened, and that's what you continue to tell yourself each time something goes wrong in your life.

For you, life started out horribly, and it's been that way since your beginning. Is there any reason for you to believe that it will ever be different? There comes a time when you no longer have hope. You start to see life as this dismal display of all the ways things will never be good for you. Nothing good will ever happen for you. If it's bad, then it'll always come your way. Were you put on this Earth to exist in misery? Yes! That must be the answer! Your life is the example to everyone around you about how God treats those He sees as having no value. To say that you feel like a stepchild is an understatement.

It's hard to have self-worth when all you see is doom when you look at the path your life has taken. The Bible says, *"You are altogether beautiful, my darling, there is no flaw in you"* (Song of Solomon 4:7). Could that be referring to you, too? Or is it just for everyone else? If there is no flaw in me, why is it that I keep making all these mistakes? Why do I keep drawing people who only want to hurt me?

It's so hard to feel good about who you are when you've heard the opposite most of your life. How can you change yourself so that you attract good people in your life? I'm not just talking about men, but good friends or people who want to play a positive role on the stage of your life. One day, it was like a light bulb came on in my head: If I kept thinking the same way, how could I expect anything to be different? Since our thoughts become our actions, then I needed to change the way I thought. That wasn't something that would be easy to do because, for over 30 years, I had looked at my reflection in the mirror and told myself the same negative things such as, *"You're never going to be enough."* Others had shown me that over and over, so why should I believe anything to the contrary? They must have seen something in me that I didn't. The problem is that even if everyone in the world is saying the same things about me, if it doesn't line up with what **GOD** says, it doesn't matter. I need to toss those thoughts aside and look to *HIM*. He says I'm beautiful, so that's what I'll believe. I knew I needed to look to God for validation, not man.

When we constantly look at flawed human beings to find out who we are or why we were created, we will always come up short. It was never their responsibility to define us.

That role only belongs to our Heavenly Father. What we must understand is that the more we run to humans, the more lost we will get and the farther away from our purpose they will take us.

What does God say about me? He says I'm the apple of His eye! That statement right there holds so much truth, joy, and peace. Why? Because if I had known to start there so many years ago, it wouldn't have mattered if others saw my value. I wouldn't have cared if they loved me enough. I would've found everything I needed in Him — the One who created me!

HE says I'm enough!

HE says I'm called!

HE says I'm chosen!

When we start there and work outward, we will make sure everything that comes our way lines up with what God says about us. All these other statements will then come into play whenever we start to doubt who we are. You see, if we first connect ourselves to the "True Vine," we won't walk around as broken shells of ourselves.

I used to say that I left the gate flawed. I never really had a chance to start this walk the right way. The problem with that train of thought is this: **IT'S NOT TRUE!** God knew the things I would encounter in my younger years. He knew the pains I would go through. He was aware of the struggles I would face. He also knew the people who would cross my path and leave broken pieces of my heart scattered all around me. In all His wisdom, He knew **WHAT** I'd need and **WHO** I'd need in life to help me along the way.

As I reflect on my journey, I can see the people God sent to guide me back to Him whenever I took a wrong turn. I know my Godmother was placed in my life — at my very beginning — to give me the foundation I would need to draw on during integral times when I'd want to give up. Admittedly, there were times when I got lost and walked away from Him.

> *"Train up a child in the way he should go; and when he is old, he will not depart from it."*
> **Proverbs 22:6**

That verse is a narrative of my life. I had the Word of God planted in me at an early age; therefore, although I strayed, I eventually returned to Him. Even during times when I ran from Him, He continued to call my name. He never gave up on me or wrote me off as a lost cause.

I'm so glad God saw something in me, even when no one else did. I think about all the times we look at the status of someone's life and make a judgment that they are beyond help. We say, *"There's nothing else we can do for them."* How is it so easy to dismiss what a person can become? It's often because we've forgotten where we started. Sometimes, we forget the gutters He pulled us out of.

We must always remember: If it weren't for the grace of God, every one of us would **still** be on the path to destruction.

Mirror Images

Merriam-Webster defines a mirror image as *"an image or object that is identical in form to another, but with the structure reversed, as in a mirror."* Another definition states it is *"a person or thing that closely resembles another."* As I write this book, I'm reminded of my own life journey and how closely it resembles that of my mother's. It was a realization that came to me only as I've been going through this writing process.

One thing I've realized is that abuse of any kind is still abuse. Whether it's physical, sexual, psychological, financial, or verbal, it's abuse. One type isn't any less harmful to an individual's mind than another. Perpetrators of abuse use the same methods to trap their victims. One of their first actions is to isolate you from everyone you know. That ensures you are dependent upon them to the point that you push others away. You are left feeling they are all you need.

I don't know if my mother would've considered herself to be an abused woman or if she just thought she was the victim of unfortunate events. I don't even remember that new man hitting her or even verbally abusing her, but he did abuse her psychologically and financially. Since she had a history of physical abuse in her past, like me, she may have felt like his behavior was okay since he wasn't hitting her. Sometimes, you're not even aware of what someone is doing to you until years after you've left the situation. As I look back on our lives during that time, I can see the same signs in her actions and behavior as I saw in my own.

Whether she was a textbook example of an abused woman or she was borderline abused, it looks and feels the same. We were dependent on the resources of a man who had complete control of our lives. It's as if I followed the same path as my mother. **Generational curses continue to occur if the cycle isn't broken.**

So many of my decisions were made because of a need, as were hers. I didn't make wise choices because I wasn't being led by anything other than a need to survive. I did whatever I needed to do to ensure the survival of my children and me. Many of my choices were made without thought for tomorrow. Instead, I focused my attention on the current circumstances or situation.

"For those who are led by the Spirit of God are the children of God."
Romans 8:14

I can't say I had a relationship with God at that time. Neither can I say I was living an overcoming life. Life was more about surviving than thriving. I couldn't see past each day or think about the next because there were days when I wasn't sure we'd have our most basic needs met. That is what caused me to run back to the man who had done everything short of killing me. The voice inside my head convinced me that it was better to endure being broken down daily rather than watching my children go without the things they had a right to such as food, shelter, clothing, etc. Was that the reason my mother stayed in her situation so long? Maybe it was the reason she went from one bad situation to one that was even worse for her and us.

When you're searching for something, you reach for anything that will carry you to the next moment. Decisions are made that may not be the best for you in the long run, but they work for the moment. I know the shame of not being able to protect my children from the pain of existing in this world. I understand what it means to sacrifice myself and my needs to make sure my children were in a good place. They are decisions a mother shouldn't have to make, but we do so because we love our children.

Oftentimes, we say, *"I'd **never** do 'this' or 'that,'"* but until you're put in a position of desperation, you can't really say for sure what you'd be willing to do. There are things I've done and choices I've made that I never thought I'd **EVER** do, but I did them because of a need to survive. I used to carry shame for those things, but I've come to realize that at the time, I did what I felt I had to do. I needed security for us all, and if it meant me living in pain, then that's what I had to do. Too many times, doing what we have to do to provide for our children becomes our mantra when it doesn't have to be. The sad thing is when you're backed into a corner and don't feel you have any other options available, you undergo things you never should've experienced. We think there's no one out there who will take a chance on us. We don't believe we're worth going to the ends of the Earth for, so we carry the load alone.

I walked the path I had chosen for myself. Making sure my children were provided for superseded all else. How often do we, as mothers, go without so our children can have more? I'm not talking about the mothers who buy their children name-brand clothing and shoes so they can fit in with the other children in the neighborhood. I'm referring to the mom who only owns one bra because she knows if she buys more for herself, she won't be able to afford that pack of socks or undershirts her children need to get through the winter months. **TRUE NEED** is what I'm referencing here. For so long, I was that mother, but I kept it hidden from those around me. I didn't want anyone to see that I was struggling to keep it together.

There are so many parallels between my story and the life of my mother, but I chose to do something different. My life took a different turn than hers because I decided to look up. In no way am I judging my mother for her life choices. I am simply pointing out the difference in our experiences. Since I am acquainted with the difficulties of raising children and being a single parent, I know that no decision is ever easy. We do the best we can with what we have. Sometimes, that works out; other times, it doesn't. I only know that God placed people in my path to help me see there was a better way. I can't say if my mother was given the same opportunity. That's her story to tell…and this is mine.

The chapters in my story involved facing the giants of my past, moving toward the future, and facing life head-on. Yes, it was scary, but I knew the generational curses my family had been subjected to over so many decades had to stop. It was up to me to do something different. I could continue to make excuses for why I couldn't do it, or I could make a change that would affect not only my own life but also the lives of my children. If I wanted a brighter future for them, there was no other choice for me to make.

I didn't want the lives of my children to look like mine. I wanted them to be overcomers. I wanted them to make choices that were part of God's plan for their lives.

> *"For as many as are led by the Spirit of God;
> they are the sons of God."*
> **Romans 8:14**

My life was filled with pitfalls and wrong turns, all because I had no direction. Although I knew of God, I didn't truly **KNOW** Him. I depended on my own thoughts and feelings to determine the path I would take. I wanted my children to follow the things of God and to have a relationship with Him — one that would prevent them from mishaps, such as the ones I encountered. I knew they wouldn't be perfect and wouldn't always make the right decisions, but I also knew they'd have a better chance of doing the right thing if they were on a Godly path.

Whether you live for God or not, everyone makes mistakes; however, having a relationship with Him makes navigating around the potholes easier. It also gives us direction. As He orders our steps and directs our path, we are being guided by His Spirit instead of our own thoughts. There are days when I wish I had known God at a young age. I am envious of my children in that way. They endured many hardships growing up, but it forced them to turn to Him at an early age. They clung to Him for survival. If I've shown them anything worthwhile, it's that He is everything they need. Nothing else matters if they don't know their Heavenly Father. When they searched for answers to why life was hard, I directed them to the only One who could comfort them. On the days they wanted to give up, I reminded them that they had a special purpose.

Although there are many similarities in my life and that of my mother, I was blessed with something different because of my foundation. God knew I would need my Godmother to set me on a course to collide with Him. He knew about all the dark nights I'd experience and the days when I would want to give up. He even knew there would be that one desperate day when I'd say to myself, *"It's all or nothing."* I wandered through life, searching for that one thing to fill the emptiness I felt inside, and then, one day, I returned to what I had been taught as a child. His Word had been planted in my heart at an early age, but as life "happened," I lost sight of who I was and who He created me to be. God's Word **NEVER** lies. One day, I returned to Him, and the generational curse no longer influenced my children or me.

Battle Scars

One day, I was watching a show called "Arrow" with my husband, Kenneith. It is one of his favorite programs, so I sometimes watch it with him to spend time together. In one of the scenes, the main characters were comparing their battle scars. They each pointed to scars on different parts of their bodies and told how they got it. One had a scar from a bullet; another had several scars from knife wounds; the third had scars from a near-death experience.

They were all so caught up in their comparisons and feeling proud of their battle wounds, none of them noticed the look on the face of the fourth character. They didn't see how much she felt left out. She had no scars to share. There were no stories for her to tell that would glorify her wounds. They were having a conversation she was unable to participate in. As she listened to them joyfully discuss their adventures, she felt isolated from them. She had no stories and nothing to show. It was as if she'd never been through anything big enough to gloat about. She could probably mention the time her heart was broken or the time her best friend walked out of her life, but there was no physical scar she could show for those things. She couldn't show them an x-ray of her heart being broken into a million pieces because of the words someone uttered to her. As she listened to their conversation, she felt like she'd never been through anything traumatic enough to leave a visible mark...at least not one worthy of comparison.

That is how it is with us as Christians. We compare our scars to those of others and measure our battles against theirs.

We say to ourselves, *"I've endured more harsh things than them."* We hold up our experiences with pride to show everyone what we've endured as if they're trophies on a shelf for all to view. We want people to look at them and be in awe of what we've endured. We think, *"No one has been through what I've been through, so others will be amazed when they hear my story. They'll comment and say how strong I am!"* Instead of using our story to encourage others, we've reduced it to something that has no value to anyone but ourselves. When we get into the habit of measuring our battles against those of others, we risk losing our place.

"Each one should test their own actions. Then, they can take pride in themselves alone, without comparing themselves to someone else, for each one should carry their own load."
Galatians 6:4-5

    Instead of revealing our scars as a way of bragging about what we've endured, we're supposed to use them to show others what God did for us. That will give them confidence that He'll do it for them as well. It's a way of uplifting others amid their battles. They should be able to look at our lives and be encouraged by the victories God has given us. The Bible says that God is not a respecter of persons, so if He did it for us, then they will know He'll do it for them, too!

    The things we've survived are not just about us; they are for **everyone** who crosses our path. Our testimony will not only help us heal but will cause others to seek healing as well. The people God places in our path aren't there by coincidence; they are placed in our lives so that we can lead them to Him.

I recognize that everything I've gone through wasn't for nothing because God doesn't waste any of our experiences. The good, the bad, and the ugly things we endure are all part of our story. They are the things that have made us who we are today.

"All things work together for the good, to them that love God and are called according to His purpose."
Romans 8:28

Nothing is **ever** lost if we choose to follow the path God has set before us.

I often wondered why I had to go through certain things. Why did God allow those horrific things to happen to me? We sometimes get so caught up in self-pity because of the pain we've gone through. Instead of using those occurrences to help others see they, too, can make it, we whine and complain about how hard our lives have been. We allow "life" to discourage us. I can say that because it used to be my daily mantra.

For many years, I sang the same old song. I complained to God about the things I went through as a child and then, as an adult. I told Him all the reasons why my life was horrible. I didn't understand why others had it so easy. I constantly questioned why I couldn't have a carefree life. I couldn't see that the things I endured had made me stronger. Yes, they were hard, but they helped me to be an **overcomer**.

As I look back on the abuse of my childhood and the damage I experienced as an adult, I now realize it's **ALL** part of my story. The amazing thing is that God is using all these things as tools. They are tools He's given me to speak encouragement into others. They are tools for me to help guide other women to a place of healing and freedom. Instead of complaining about my battle scars, I've learned to embrace them and use them as a banner of victory!

If my life had no struggles, I wouldn't truly appreciate the life God has blessed me with. That's right; I said **BLESSED!** The presence of problems or struggles doesn't mean I'm not blessed; it means I've come through some things. I haven't just come through them; I've done so victoriously!

When we go through battles, as long as we come out on the other side, it's a **WIN!** We may have scars, but we're stronger. It's that strength that will take us through the next battle and allow us to come out as the victor. Despite the bruises and being banged up, we made it!

You are a winner! That's what you can tell yourself each time you overcome a situation.

Soul Ties

How many relationships have you been in? — a question *many* of us would be too embarrassed to answer. Either we'd dodge it or try to deflect and change the subject. I will admit: There was a time in my life when I would've done the same thing. There's a lot of shame that comes with admitting we have no idea how many faces we've seen or how many times we've given ourselves away to someone who had no right to have a part of us. I don't talk about it much because there's a temptation to feel shame for not having that **ONE** lasting marriage.

When we've been sexually active with others, we develop lasting bonds with them. These are called "Soul Ties." According to Tim Steward in *Soul Ties and Breaking Soul Ties*, a soul tie is defined as *"a spiritual connection between two people who have been physically intimate with each other or who have had an intense emotional or spiritual association or relationship."* After a while, physical intimacy becomes as easy as drinking a glass of water. You become numb to things that are going on in your life and no longer care what happens to you. It wasn't like I was a prize to be possessed, so it didn't matter if I was no longer pure. Once you've allowed so many to use you, there's no more pretending it matters.

"Who can find a virtuous woman? For her price is far above rubies."
Proverbs 31:10

How could I see myself as a virtuous woman, knowing all the things I've allowed myself to be subjected to? I felt both worthless and unworthy of anything good. Could this God who called me a 'virtuous woman' love me? What does He see when He looks down upon my face? Does He see all the stains?

One thing that happens when you allow others to take pieces of you is that there comes a time when you have nothing left. You're depleted to the point that you are bankrupt of anything that you used to be.

As for me, I had **nothing** left inside and didn't know how to move forward with who I was. After years of doing the same thing and hoping the "next man" would see my value, I had come to a point where I didn't want to do this anymore. I was tired of expecting something different in each new face. I just wanted to be loved. I wanted someone to look at me and see who I could be.

The first time a man touched me, the message he sent to my young mind was that I was created for his pleasure. It didn't matter what his touch did to me. It didn't matter how it made me feel. Neither did it matter to him how it broke everything inside me. From that first touch to the next one and the next one, each additional man told me I was there for the taking to serve his insatiable needs.

I began to see myself as an object rather than a person. I was only valuable for my body and nothing else. The fact that I was smart meant nothing to anyone I encountered *(at least that was the message I continued to receive loud and clear)*. There were so many times I silently cried because I wanted just **ONE** of them to see the real me. I was more than a warm body to lay with at night. I needed to know that my life meant more than what I had been given up to that point.

Soul ties don't just take away something from you physically. They're also a mental and spiritual stripping away of who you are. There are no deposits made; only withdrawals. You don't realize how much is being taken away until it's too late. One day, you look in the mirror and hate the person staring back at you. You no longer recognize who she is. You're ashamed of what you've become. No one wants an overused woman who doesn't even love herself! All the signs told me I would never be anything.

I felt empty! To whom could I run to for comfort? Where could I go to be made whole again? Despite the number of times I went to God for help, I always left His presence feeling like I had failed yet again. I continued to try to be what I was supposed to be. I wanted to be flawless like everyone else, but I kept falling.

"For a just man falleth seven times, and riseth up again..."
Proverbs 24:16

No matter how deep we are in sin, God is always there waiting for us to come to Him.

I didn't have to continue feeling like a nobody. I had tried too many times to fill the emptiness with men or things, only to end up broken. Then, one day, God reminded me of my foundation. He reminded me that He is the only one who can love me the way I needed and deserved to be loved.

"You are altogether beautiful, my darling; there is no flaw in you."
Song of Solomon 4:7

It doesn't matter how many times I've been married or how many times I've looked for love in all the wrong places because God loves me despite my flaws.

If we're honest, how many of us have had these feelings? How many times have we looked to someone or something else to sum up the whole of who we are? It's time to stop allowing others to define us. It's time to look to **GOD!**

PRAYER:

God, help me to seek You to find out who I am. Help me to not look to people or things to define who You say that I am. Give me strength on those days when I am weak, and help me to turn to You. I know that I am your most prized possession.
Amen.

The Vision

I remember the scene like it was yesterday. As it entered my mind, it came across like a movie. I could hear the voice, and it sounded like my own. There were so many women in the room. It was filled from the front to the back, and they were all focused on the person at the podium. The room was beautiful, reminding me of the locations I had visited whenever I attended conferences or gatherings for some type of seminar.

I was confused at first because I didn't understand what I was seeing or why. At the time, I was sitting in our living room, wondering how my children and I would get back to the United States. We were thousands of miles away from home, with an ocean separating us from everyone we loved. How did I allow myself to come this far? Germany was a long way to go to save a marriage I already knew was ending. I had just been told my ex-husband's military unit believed we needed to go through counseling. In their opinion, I was homesick and needed to get out more into the community to find things that would make me feel less lonely.

That was the night *after* he tried to take my life. I'd gone through all the required steps of reporting the incident. The police report was filed, leaving me sitting silently with a restraining order in my hand. Everyone was aware of his attempt to kill me, yet they felt that since he was a great soldier, the "incident" was something we could overcome. They believed counseling would help us work through our issues. There was no need to break up the family. It didn't matter to them that it wasn't the first time. They had seen the previous police reports in the system, but that wasn't enough to convince them that the problem was bigger than me being homesick.

I felt stuck! What was I going to do now? How would I get us back home? The plan I had originally come up with wouldn't work now. I had to go back to the drawing board and rethink everything. Although I had no clue, God did!

> *"For I know the plans I have for you, declares the Lord,*
> *plans to prosper you and not to harm you,*
> *plans to give you a hope and a future."*
> **Jeremiah 29:11**

I knew it was time for me to walk out of that life. I also knew I had done everything I could to make the marriage work. I realized there was nothing else I could do. It wasn't my responsibility to save him. I couldn't continue to stand in the gap and wait for him to be the man I wanted him to be. Life wasn't just about me; it was also about my children who were looking at the damage that was being done daily. They had a front-row seat to the nightmare that had become our life. If I didn't get out of the destructive lifestyle for myself, I had to do it for them.

I made a mistake early in our marriage of thinking my love would be enough to make him want to change. I thought I could motivate him to be better. Then, once we started having children, I thought they would be what he needed. The problem is that I wanted the marriage to work more than he did. Each time we got into an altercation, he reminded me that he was only doing this for our children and me. **Real change only comes when**

you really want it. It comes from within a person. Since he didn't think there was anything wrong with his behavior, the change was always temporary. It would only be a matter of time before he reverted to his old ways.

As I sat in that dark room, I realized that although I didn't know how it would happen, God would get us back to where we needed to be. I believe that is why He gave me that vision so many years ago. It wasn't just about my future or the plan He had for my life "one day"; it was also about the situation I found myself in that dreadful night. The vision was a glimpse into where He was preparing to take me. It was also to give me hope for the future that was to come. God knew I would need something to hold on to because there would be challenging and discouraging times ahead.

Sometimes, the journey before us has rough terrain, but God gives us what we need at the moment to prepare us. When God gives us snapshots of things to come, we don't always understand what He's showing us until He makes the picture clear in His time. In the interim, He continues to give us clues along our journey as we need them for encouragement and motivation to keep going.

"Now we see things imperfectly, like puzzling reflections in a mirror, but then we will see everything with perfect clarity. All that I know now is partial and incomplete, but then I will know everything completely, just as God now knows me completely."
1 Corinthians 13:12

I was given that vision in 2007, but there was a **long** journey ahead of me and **many** dark times to walk through. At different points in my life since then, God has renewed the vision and reminded me of what He told me. It was during my darkest days that I had to reflect on that night and remind myself that He gave me a dream and it would come to pass. I saw myself standing in front of hundreds of women, speaking words of encouragement over them. It was something I know that only God could do in my life.

I was a woman who had never felt led to speak to the masses, but I knew if God showed it to me, then it was going to come to pass. There are times when I look back on that night and reflect on how far I've come. It has only been by the grace of God that I didn't give up. When we're given something from the Father, it's important that we hold onto it tightly because there will be days when we want to throw it all away. It gets hard, and we get tired, but we must continue to walk the path He has set before us.

Although I only had a glimpse of my future, it was on that day the dream began for me. I knew there was a special purpose for my life. I believed that God was going to use me in a mighty way. I just had to go through the process and be obedient to what He had given me. He trusted me with this path, and He has been taking me through the process since that night.

Has God given you a vision? What about a dream or plan for your life? I believe each of us has something God has given us to do. I also believe each of us has an assignment to fulfill that only we can do. There are people in our path who are waiting for us to do what He has placed on our hearts to do.

We can't shrink back or allow fear to stop us from moving forward. The dream is too important for us to allow it to fall by the wayside.

No matter what you've gone through in your past or what you're experiencing in your present, you can do anything God has called you to do.

"I can do all things through Christ who strengthens me."
Philippians 4:13

Read that verse again, but this time, read it aloud and insert your name. Whenever I read that verse, I make it personal to me:

"Tyria can do ALL things through Christ who strengthens her."

I know it may sound strange talking about myself in the third person, but I do that sometimes. It's my way of giving myself a pep talk. I use whatever is needed to keep me focused on the path ahead.

What are some ways you keep yourself on track? If you're not sure where you're going, I suggest that you seek God for the answers. He is your Creator; therefore, He has the plan for you to follow. No matter what He has for you to do, believe that it is possible. If He can use a divorced, single mother with no hopes of a future, He can use you, too! Just allow Him to pour everything into you that He has and walk in the purpose He lays before you.

When God gives us a vision for our lives, it's sometimes difficult to believe. We may not feel that it is something we're capable of doing. Maybe we're looking at ourselves through a tainted view. We're seeing ourselves in the present form—where we are now—instead of where we're going or what we can be.

That day, as I sat in that dark room, I never thought I'd write one book, much less four or five. I'm glad God sees my beginning and my end and knows my life story.

On that dark day, He took something that was **broken** and made it into a *beautiful* story for the world to see. I didn't know then that it was the beginning of a new life for my children and me. He began a **NEW** thing in me that very day!

There's No Shame

There were many times when I worked up the courage and poured my heart out to a friend because I had had enough. I wanted **OUT!** I didn't want to live that life any longer. The result of that conversation I had envisioned in my head didn't turn out to be my reality. Most of the time, I was met with disbelief. *"He couldn't possibly be doing all the horrible things you're accusing him of doing!"* It must be me! I wasn't the wife I needed to be for him because he was a good man, a great husband, and an excellent father to his children. I should be ashamed of myself for saying such things about him.

If it wasn't the shame of not being good enough in the eyes of those who loved him, it was the shame I felt from others who felt I should've left a long time ago. There was shame coming at me from all sides and for different reasons. I began to feel it and direct it inward. Shame is defined as *"a painful feeling of humiliation or distress caused by the consciousness of wrong or foolish behavior."* Why was I feeling shame? Why did I readily accept it and allow others to place it on me? I had done nothing wrong. **I was the victim!**

When a woman is abused, she is beaten down to the point that she has no fight left in her. When he tells her it's her fault, she easily believes it. She no longer has it in her to reason it away or reject the notion. At the point when others begin to assign shame to her, it's the same. She's being revictimized repeatedly by people who have no idea they are doing so. It's unfathomable to them that he could be this monster because they do not see it in him. It alleviates their guilt by placing it all back in the victim's lap. They couldn't possibly have missed the signs. It must not be true. Or she must've done something to cause him to act out of character.

What we must realize is that it takes a lot for a woman to get to the point of confiding in another. She is fearful that if she tells the wrong person, it may get back to him. What if she trusts the wrong person? Not only must she face their shame; her abuser's wrath once they're behind closed doors awaits. He will punish her for betraying him to the people they love. He will remind her that it is her job to have his back, even though he's never had hers. It's up to her to keep the family together. She takes it all in and promises to do better. She tells him all the things he expects to hear. She must reassure him that she is all in for him!

The night my ex-husband tried to take my life was like all the previous ones. I uttered all the things I knew would calm him down. I wanted to make sure he believed I wanted the best for him. I needed to convince him that being his wife was a joy for me, so I apologized for the betrayals. I reassured him I had no plans of ever leaving him. In the years and days before, I would've meant all the words I spoke. He had a way of making me see the error of my ways whenever thoughts of escaping came to my mind.

The difference that time was that I no longer carried the shame of staying in a toxic relationship. I wanted to make myself a priority. I knew that no matter what opposition I faced, it was what I needed to do. That night, I made the conscious decision to push forward with my safety plan, no matter who was for or against me doing so. The women who get to that point are often determined to speak their truth to whoever will listen. They've built a "thick skin" and are prepared for all the people who will stand in disbelief of their story. They are ready for those who will ask the question, *"Why?"* They have steeled their emotions because they know the onslaught is coming. They also understand that even if there is not one person in their corner, they can no longer carry the shame and guilt of being a battered woman.

Those same women know they must transform themselves from *victim* to *survivor* to an *overcomer*. I was that woman! As I speak my truth daily and empower other women to share their truths, I am reminded that it didn't happen overnight for me. It was and still is an everyday battle to remind myself of who I am. I'm constantly reminding myself that my past doesn't determine who I am today.

There was a time when I was afraid to share with the world all the times I had allowed my abuser to beat me down. I didn't want to hear that I was weak for staying. I didn't want others to look down on me for loving him. I didn't know how to stand up to him or stand up for myself whenever confronted with the ugly words from others. Now, I **DO**! Today, I am a different person—all because I let go of the *SHAME*.

It took a lot of work on my part to release the shame. I had to look in the mirror and admit some things to myself. In a toxic relationship, we each must admit the part we played. I had to admit that I allowed myself to be treated as less than the woman God created me to be. I also had to understand why it happened. What was missing inside me that caused me to accept that behavior from him? Why didn't I value who I was?

In all the searching, I realized I didn't like who I was. I met him at a time when I was vulnerable. It was as if there was a beacon inside me that led him straight to me. He picked up on all my insecurities and understood that he'd be able to use them against me. I'm not saying he set out to abuse me in the beginning, but I do believe once it started, he took my weaknesses and used them to his advantage to further break me down. I've heard the expression, *"Knowing is half the battle!"* That was so true for me.

Once I understood, I knew I needed help. I began to take steps to make myself better and stronger. I worked on my insecurities and committed to doing the work it would take to be whole. In my situation, I had left him before, only to go back after years of being free. I realized I did so because I had refused to address my issues. Instead, I chose to blame him for it all and not accept any personal responsibility. This time around was different.

The most important thing about moving forward was knowing there was no more shame. ***I could do this!***

Escaping the Pain

How do you move on when you've dealt with so much heartache and pain? Where does it all go? Pain is a funny thing. It affects everyone differently. Some use it as a vehicle to take them throughout their life. They hold on to the pain and use it as their fuel to get them through the memories. It carries them through life as they use it to shut out their feelings. They become numb. They bury all thoughts and memories associated with the pain and operate as if it doesn't exist.

Conversely, others allow the pain to paralyze them and cause them to give up on everything. They go throughout each day not living their dreams and avoiding anything that will cause them to possibly face that type of pain again. Their mindset is that if they do nothing, then they can avoid getting hurt again. They don't allow anyone into their life for fear of encountering disappointment. *"Why hope for anything if I'll only lose anyway?"* That's the **negative** self-talk that plays in their head daily. They've allowed the fear of feeling the pain again to stop them from living life to the fullest. Both are unhealthy and ineffective ways of overcoming and healing from whatever it is that caused the hurt. We must face it head-on and deal with everything that comes with it if we desire complete healing.

When a turtle feels threatened, it retreats into its shell. That's the way it protects itself from danger. Since the turtle can't move quickly, the shell serves as a secure barrier against whatever may try to cause harm. The way I chose to deal with my pain was like that of the turtle. Instead of facing it head-on,

I chose to hide within myself. When the pain was too much, I wanted to escape and avoid what I was feeling inside. Instead of standing and fighting, I would run in the opposite direction.

There are so many ways we may choose to conquer the overload of emotions. What if there was a pill that would allow us to remove all the pain or an app that would erase the parts of our past that we no longer wanted to exist? How many of us would welcome that solution? Although this seems to be an appealing way to cope with it all, there are many reasons why it wouldn't be wise.

If we erase parts of our life that we don't like or take a pill to remove the bad memories and pain, what would we be left with? We would also be taking away good things in our lives. I used to think that maybe if I hadn't married my children's fathers, then my life would've turned out different. It would've been better *(or I would've made wiser decisions)*. But would I have the same children? The thing about life is that you must take the good along with the bad. My children are the best things that have happened in my life, besides marrying my current husband. Even in the pain, my children have brought me so much joy. They are worth all the hard times I've lived through, and I wouldn't trade my life for another if it meant not having them.

There are things or situations we encounter that we struggle to come to terms with. We don't understand why "it" happened. Why us? Why couldn't our lives have taken a different turn? Once we realize there is a purpose in everything we experience, we'll stop asking those questions. I no longer ask, *"Why?"* Instead, I ask, *"**How can my pain be used to spare someone else from the same experience? How can I show others they, too, can overcome whatever obstacles they face? What can I do to support someone else's journey to wholeness?**"*

It's amazing how different the world looks once we stop focusing on ourselves. Once we realize everything isn't about us and what we're going through, we become free to live the life God purposed for us. We're no longer bound by self-pity and defeat. Instead, we're constantly reaching out to see how many others we can bring along on the journey toward freedom in Christ. I think about all the years I wasted wallowing in my own junk; the years when I refused to deal with past hurt resulting from the childhood abuse. Who knows how my life would've been had I decided to trust God with my healing and do so sooner rather than years later?

"He heals the brokenhearted and binds up their wounds."
Psalm 147:3

Whenever we're troubled, scared, or broken from what we've encountered in life, God is there to usher us into the healing of our wounds. Whenever I was upset about something and just wanted to be alone, a friend of mine used to say, *"No one cries alone. I'll cry with you."* It's the same with God. He doesn't want us to cry alone. He desires that we bring it all to Him and lay it at His feet. It is there that we find comfort. Once we've had an encounter with Him, we will have a peace that passes all understanding.

Now, I'm not saying the wounds disappear, but He doesn't leave us to ourselves to just "deal with it." He feels our pain and wants us to come to Him. Whether we decide to bring our cares to Him or not, He knows we are hurting and waits for us with open arms. Whenever one of my children is in trouble or dealing with hard things, I do whatever I can to offer a safe place. There are times I want to take all their pain away and make all their hurts disappear, but I am human and don't have the ability to do so. All I can do is pray to God to help them. The great thing for us is that God can take our pain and make it as if it never happened.

Yes, the things we went through will still be in our past, but we won't feel the pain that was once associated with it. There will be memories, but we will be able to talk about it and not cry. There will be tears, but not sorrow. In its place, there will be an overwhelming joy!

"You have turned my mourning into dancing for me; You have taken off my sackcloth and clothed me with joy, that my soul may sing praise to You and not be silent, O Lord my God, I will give thanks to You forever."
Psalm 30:11-12

PRAYER:

God, help me to release all my pain to You. Help me to forgive those who have hurt me. I know that forgiveness is not just for them, but for me as well. "Bless those who persecute you. Don't curse them; pray that God will bless them" (Romans 12:14).
Amen.

Letting Go

Where do you even begin? You have so much baggage that you've carried around for years. Even though the weight feels so heavy, you continue to bring it along from relationship to relationship and experience to experience because it's what you're used to doing. It scares you a little to think what your life would be like without it. Sometimes, we hold onto pain because it's become a part of us, and we mistakenly believe it's who we are. Holding onto the pain will keep us from so many beautiful things that God wants to bring into our life.

When I was in basic training, we used to do ruck marches. We were required to put 50 pounds into our rucksack and go on a march for five miles with the rest of our military unit. That was one of the hardest things I've ever done in my life, but I realize I didn't have to like it to receive the benefits from it. The activity wasn't just about physical endurance; it also built our mental endurance. We carried around extra weight, which helped to make our minds and bodies stronger.

Carrying around hurt has the opposite effect on us. Instead of strengthening us, it makes us weaker in every way: spiritually, physically, and mentally. The longer we transport it around, the more detrimental it becomes to every part of our life. We've all gone through things that have threatened to take us out; things we didn't think we'd come back from. Whether you're a domestic violence survivor, a victim of childhood sexual abuse, been abused by people who said they loved you, or some other traumatic experience, that hurt was never supposed to define who you are. Instead of allowing ourselves to be broken down by past hurts, we must use those experiences to catapult us into our destiny.

It becomes so easy to "just live with it." You tell yourself, *"This is my lot in life."* You don't know how to move on like everyone keeps telling you to do. Don't they realize how much those experiences took away from you? If they had gone through what you did, then maybe they'd understand why you choose to keep your hurt close. It's what keeps you from allowing anyone else to do the same thing to you again. It protects you!

Those are often the thoughts of a wounded person. When we've been in a place for too long, we start to tell ourselves lies that will soothe us for the moment and help us get through the next day. It becomes easier to block out things that God is trying to speak to us because we just don't want to hear it. **"Let it go and give it to God!"** That's the one thing I kept hearing over and over from so many people, but if I listened to them and let it go, then the people who hurt me would get a free pass.

What does God say?

Let's take a moment to refer back to the rucksack. The contents included a variety of items that made up the 50 additional pounds we were to carry. Each item represented a tool to be used to make us **stronger** and **better**.

Just the same, God has given each of us tools to use to get us to where we're going. If we get stuck on the journey, that's when we turn those things over to Him. 1 Peter 5:7 says we are to cast our cares on Him because He cares for us. It's not His desire that we get stuck in the process. For that reason, we should look to Him for help when the pressure gets to be too much. If we do so, we'll be able to walk the path He's placed before us without being weighed down. We'll be able to do the one thing we were created to do.

As I marched with the rucksack on my back, there were moments when I felt like I couldn't move another step. The weight was just too much for me to carry. Sometimes, when a soldier was struggling during the march, another would come alongside her to offer a little motivation. That person was usually their "Battle Buddy." They'd motivate and encourage their buddy so they wouldn't give up. If one fell behind, the other would make sure they weren't alone. There were times when my buddy was injured, so I was required to carry her load. The same concept holds true for God. He wants to do the same for us. He wants to carry our load because He knows it's too much for us to do alone.

If we release it all, we can make it. It's that simple! No more carrying around things that we're not built to handle. The sooner we let it go, the healthier we will be. Release it, and God will take it from there!

Are there things you've been holding on to? Maybe you don't think you will know who you are if you no longer have them. Maybe you're afraid of what your life will look like with that empty space. Whatever your reason, know that **God is waiting for you** to place it all at His feet. Once you do, you'll feel instant peace. That peace will come *flooding* in. You won't understand it; you'll just know it's what you've needed and you'll wonder why you didn't let it go sooner.

TIME FOR REFLECTION
What has God asked you to surrender to Him?

PRAYER:

God, help me to surrender anything from my past that is holding me back from walking in my purpose. I give it all to You. "Therefore, if any man be in Christ, he is a new creature: old things are passed away; behold, all things are become new" (2 Corinthians 5:17).
Amen.

No More Chains

There's a song that comes to my mind by Eddie James. Part of the chorus says, *"No more shackles, no more chains, no more bondage. I am free!"* When I think about all that God has brought me through, I want to raise my hands in the air and shake them because I know I'm no longer bound. I don't have any chains on me. I used to walk around with chains on my hands and shackles on my feet. These chains had me bound, and there was no freedom. I was a slave to fear! Fear kept me in a marriage where God had no place. There was no room for God in our marriage because my husband was the ruler and master over me.

The Bible says that Hagar was a slave woman. She lived for the pleasure of her master. She wasn't free to make decisions for herself because her life didn't belong to her. She existed to please Abraham and Sarah. That was my life, as well. I lived to please my husband. That is not to be confused with the writings of Paul in 1 Corinthians 7:34 when he says, *"A married woman is concerned with the affairs of her husband and how she may please him."* My marriage was not led by God because I was living as a slave wife instead of a freeborn wife. Instead of being treated like the gift God says I am, I was treated like a piece of property. That is what Hagar was; the property of her master. She did what Abraham and Sarah instructed her to do. She could have done things she wanted to do, but in biblical times, she would've been viewed as an un-submissive slave.

When a slave gets out of line, they are usually brought back under submission through beatings. That is what my life was about. I had to always follow the rules that were set before me. If those rules weren't followed, there would be harsh consequences. In an environment such as that, it was difficult to thrive and be the vessel God created me to be. Instead of my life being about serving God and doing His will, I had chosen to surrender to my husband and submit to his will. Now that Christ is the head of my life, I know I'm no longer a slave to the things of this world — and that includes people. I don't live for others any longer.

Galatians 5:1 says, *"Christ has truly set us free!"* We are heirs to the King of kings! We are from the lineage of Sarah. We are free women who were born to do our Father's business. God gave each of us a purpose. Before I was free, I thought I had no life. I merely existed from one day to the next. Once I embraced my freedom, I knew God had a special purpose for my life that only I could fulfill. Do you realize that in the millions of people who have lived on this Earth in the past, present, and future, there will never be another you? When each of us is created, God already knows what He has designed us to do. It's something that can't be done by anyone else. **How amazing is that?**

Once God sets us free from the bondage of one relationship, we must be careful not to go that route again. We must examine our behavior and actions to get to the root of why we allow ourselves to be so easily controlled. When you've been controlled and manipulated by one person, it's so much easier to slip into that type of relationship again with someone else. It's an unhealthy tendency that you've developed, and it's something that must be broken before you can be whole.

> *"Now, make sure that you stay free,*
> *and don't get tied up again in slavery."*
> **Galatians 5:1**

Many of us get caught up in "people bondage." We live for the approval of others and seek to please them in whatever way possible. We don't realize it until we're so far in that we can't imagine how our life would be if we didn't do the things required to be happy in the relationship. I'm not talking about a marriage or even an intimate relationship. What I'm referring to is a relationship on a different level. It's the friendships that have turned into family—friends who are supposed to stick to you closer than a sister, but instead of being healthy, they've slid into the toxic side of the spectrum.

As much as it's hard to believe, some friendships cause us to be in bondage. Once I left my abusive marriage, I found myself being dominated by other relationships. The ones who started out as my help slowly became a hindrance to what God was trying to do in my life. These were the people who presented themselves as friends. I was so far away from my family, and I desperately needed to feel like I had someone in my corner. When you've had a constant breaking of your spirit, you accept the first glimmer of light that comes your way.

Those people became like family. They said and did all the things I needed at the time. It was hard not to allow them to gradually take over my life. I didn't see that it was the beginning of me allowing myself to be controlled yet again. I'd gone from one prison and walked right into another. I didn't realize what was happening, so I readily accepted the place I was in. Before I knew it, they were making all my decisions and telling me what I could and couldn't do. I hadn't seen it coming! It was too late to run or get out because I had nowhere else to go. Again, I had allowed someone other than God to be my "master."

The same feelings I experienced with my husband were the same things I felt at that moment. I felt trapped! I didn't think I would find someone else who would love me the way they did. In fact, I was often told, *"You won't ever find another friend like me!"* That was **NOT** normal! A "friend" would never say things like that. A friend who is sent by God will always want the best for your life and not wish harm upon you. They would be someone who loves you and won't be jealous when you have other friends in your life. Nonetheless, I believed what that "friend" said—just as I listened to the words of my ex-husband when he told me no one would love me like he did. I thought I would be lost without those "friends" who were now "family." It was difficult to break free from them, and it took years of healing. Once my eyes were opened and I saw clearly what was happening, I knew I had to break the chains once again.

When we keep going from toxic relationship to toxic relationship, we must recognize there is something inside us that is broken. Why do we keep doing this? What is it about us that is attracted to people who want to control and manipulate us?

I wanted so desperately to break the cycle of being unhealthy and codependent. *"Codependency is an emotional and behavioral condition that affects an individual's ability to have a healthy, mutually satisfying relationship. It is also known as "relationship addiction" because people with codependency often form or maintain relationships that are one-sided, emotionally destructive and/or abusive"* (Mental Health America, 2019).

There were more changes I needed to make, and it had to begin before I found myself in yet another unhealthy relationship. I didn't want to lose myself in someone else ever again. I began to understand that part of the problem was me being attracted to people I could fix or rescue, as well as those who could take care of me. A relationship should always be beneficial to both parties. Following are the things I did to break free:

- ❖ Took my life back
    - o Began making my own decisions
    - o Sought God to find out who I was
    - o Learned to trust myself
    - o Stopped looking to others to tell me how to feel or live my life
    - o Established healthy boundaries for my relationships
    - o Detached myself from relationships that weren't beneficial and fulfilling
    - o Built my self-esteem

When another person is controlling us, we must understand the root of the problem resides within us. A lack of self-love is usually where it starts. We don't believe we're capable of living our life on our own without someone telling us what to do. We have no confidence in our own abilities, which is the beginning of us accepting whatever they choose to do to us. We believe we deserve whatever we get, but we don't. The cycle can be broken. We can live a victorious life!

I took a long, hard look in the mirror and realized the changes had to start with me if I ever wanted to be who God called me to be. The steps weren't always easy, but I did them, and now, I can say it was all for a better version of me.

Finding Me

Maybe you aren't in bondage to a person. Perhaps it's a "thing." God sees it all the same. If He is not the King of your life, you are not free. Sometimes, we exchange one type of chain for another. God frees us from the bondage of a person, and we replace them with things or addictions. Although I was free from the bondage of relationships, there were other things God had to remove from my life to make me whole.

There was a time in my life when I didn't know who I was. During the years after I left my abusive marriage, I clung to unhealthy thoughts and feelings. I was lonely, depressed, and bitter. Although I was thankful to God for saving my life, I wondered why He did it. Was my life worth saving? What was my purpose? Others hadn't been blessed to see another day, so I questioned God about what made me different. What was so special about me that He saw fit to spare me that night? People say there's a testimony that comes forth from the things we go through, but at that time, I didn't see my life as a testimony; I saw it as a failure! I felt like a walking disaster. I was a single mother of four children with two failed marriages, no job, no hope, and no future. How could God do anything with all of that mess?

Although I had a relationship with God, I had a hard time believing what His Word said about me. I had to reprogram my thinking. I was going to church. I was even over different ministries. However, amid it all, I hated life. On the outside, I looked like I had it all together but inside, I was slowly dying. Yes, I looked like I was sold out to God, but that's because I had learned the Christian lingo. I knew what to say and do to deceive others...and myself. Whenever anyone asked me how I was doing, my response would always be the same:

"I'M BLESSED AND HIGHLY FAVORED!"

There was a problem, though. I didn't **really** believe my own words. My heart was not clean or pure. I was angry with God, and bitterness had grown in my heart. I was able to deceive everyone else, but God wasn't fooled. He knew my true condition. A part of me was even angry that He had spared my life. God knew about the secret thoughts that went through my mind the night my ex-husband almost killed me. I was so tired of living a life of pain, I had wished he would take my life. That was one time I wanted him to succeed. Yes, I loved my children, but I didn't want to feel the pain any longer. I didn't want to see it in their eyes. How many of you can admit to yourselves that there was a time when you wanted your tormentor to succeed in his efforts? If we're not honest with ourselves, we can never get to the place where we can begin to heal.

We can't continue going through each day pretending we're on top of the world when we know we're really *struggling* just to make it through another day. There were even times when I would've gladly exchanged the loneliness to be back in bondage. I complained to God daily, much like the Israelites did when God delivered them from Egypt. Instead of being grateful for God's provisions and blessings, they murmured and complained...just as I did. Like them, I had so easily forgotten what God had done for me, and I became complacent. Instead of having praise in my heart and on my lips, I blamed Him for my hardships.

I continued to blame God for the things I had gone through, even though it was all due to my poor life choices. It was me who made the decisions that led me into an abusive marriage. I chose to enter broken relationships. It wasn't God's fault, but I blamed Him for it all. It wasn't until I realized that even though I was playing the Christian role and doing all the things I was supposed to do to look the part, my heart still didn't belong to my Heavenly Father. I was still not completely submitted to Him and His will for my life. I had to get to a place of desperation. One day, God brought me to a breaking point. I decided to serve Him with my whole heart, mind, body, and soul. I no longer wanted to "play the part." I wanted to be true to who God said I was.

When I allowed God to be King in every area of my life, I began to see things differently. I had a new perspective! Instead of complaining, I rejoiced in all things. I gave God praise for all He had done for me. Instead of seeking a relationship or a man, I allowed God to be those things for me, too. I set my mind on the things above and not on fleshly things. When we allow God to lead us in all things, He will give sweet surprises.

That's what He did for me with Kenny. I wasn't looking for a relationship. I didn't' even want to be married again. But God said, *"YES!"* The difference between this marriage and my previous marriages is that I am the daughter of Sarah. I am a freeborn wife. My husband treats me like a gift. He knows that he has God's favor and is blessed beyond measure because I belong to him.

> *"The man who finds a wife finds a treasure,*
> *and he receives favor from the Lord."*
> **Proverbs 18:22**

I used to wonder what my purpose was. I now know that my purpose was **always** in my story. **Each of us has a story to tell.** Each of us has someone God wants us to reach and lead to Him. People are waiting for us to be obedient and do what He has called us to do. If we allow fear to cause us to shrink back, we'll not only miss the blessings God has in store for our lives, but we'll also delay what He wants to do in the lives of those on our path.

I can now look at the things I've been through and, instead of allowing them to make me sad or angry, **I REJOICE!** I know that it was all for a good purpose. That may sound strange. It may sound as if I'm saying I wanted to go through the heartache and abuse, but it's exactly the opposite. No, I'm not happy I experienced the harshness of living through an abusive marriage, but the fact that I can say, *"I* **LIVED** *through it,"* is something to be thankful for. Now, I get to go out and show everyone around me the amazingness of God and how He brought me out.

I've often said, *"I don't look like what I've been through."* God has redeemed the years I lost during that time as He has restored me. I know He can and will do it for you…if you would allow Him.

Marriage is the Cure

When Kenneith came into my life, God told me he was going to be my husband. Even still, I had doubts because of past things. Although I felt peace about marrying him, I went into my new marriage with so many insecurities. I didn't know if I could be a good wife. I had failed at this twice and didn't possess the confidence that this time would be different. Yes, I knew God brought him to me, but was I different? I wanted an assurance that the problem wasn't me.

My first husband used to tell me all the time that it was me who caused the monster inside him to come out. The person inside me knew that wasn't the truth; it was a problem he had to work out. Still, a small voice remained that said, *"Maybe he was right."* I then thought about how my second marriage had failed. He wasn't a terrible husband, and I knew that if he hadn't been bound by the drugs, maybe our marriage would've worked.

Now, here I was on my ***third*** marriage. When you've failed so much, you start to wonder if it's worth even trying to be successful anymore. When Kenneith and I had to complete the application for our marriage license, we had to put the number of previous marriages. That has always been an embarrassment for me. It was my mark of shame. It told everyone that I was no good at anything; therefore, I was a failure. It's a constant reminder of how many times I've gotten it wrong.

The thing I am constantly reminding myself of is that my experiences don't define who I am. I've bungled up so many things in my life, but they are just that and nothing more. I can't allow those mess-ups—no matter how numerous they are—to stop me from doing the things I know I've been called to do.

I couldn't enter this marriage being led by thoughts of failing. If I did that, then I would be failing before I even began. I was defeating myself without even trying to see this as different. Instead of looking at this marriage as a new beginning or a new start, I had already lumped it together with the other two. I had so easily forgotten that this marriage was different from the others.

It wasn't me who put myself with Kenny. **God brought us together!** I had been healed and made whole. Instead of jumping into another relationship (as I had done in the past), I gave myself to God. I did it the right way this time around, so I wasn't going in blindly. He was for me, and I was for him.

Why, then, was I allowing myself to be defeated in my thoughts?

Our thoughts affect our actions. Whatever we think will usually be what we end up doing. If I told myself enough that my marriage was condemned, then I would start to see it through flawed lenses.

"For as a man thinketh in his heart, so is he…"
Proverbs 23:7

That is not the path I wanted to take. I knew I had the wrong mindset. I couldn't focus on my failures. I was making everything about me, and it wasn't.

Kenny and I had had many discussions about what our marriage would represent. We knew it was all about God and that everything we did would have God as the primary focus. So, if our marriage was about God, then there was no room for me to insert my thoughts. During our marriage counseling, we were required to come up with a mission statement—something we both wanted to see in our marriage. To this day, it's something we've continued to adhere to:

- To love each other like no one else has ever done.
- To always make him feel like the king of his castle and her feel like the queen of her home.
- To support each other 100% in everything we do, so that we always know we have someone on our side, even when no one else is.
- We will do this with love and respect for each other.

That mission statement is placed on our bathroom wall. We each look at it daily to remind us that our union isn't about him or me; it's about God. That is what it means to have a marriage God's way. When you take the focus off yourself and come together as one, you're able to walk in your joint purpose. Your marriage is not about you individually, but what God will do through you as a single unit. We pledged to always keep Christ at the center of everything we do. When you keep yourself out of the equation, it's easy to serve the purpose God has placed on you, both **individually** and as **a couple**.

The day Kenny proposed ended up being a beautiful day, even though it didn't start out that way. I thought the day would go one way, but God, Kenny, and everyone else knew different. By the end of the day, I was wearing an engagement ring and having a romantic dinner with the love of my life. That day turned out a lot different than I thought it would. It wasn't "just another day"; it was one of the happiest days of my life!

That's how life often presents itself. Although we plan, there is always a chance that things won't go according to what we expect. I entered my marriage thinking it would be the cure for all the bad things I'd experienced in my past. I felt like Kenny was the answer to all my prayers. Here I was, 40 years old and just beginning my life. The day I walked down the aisle was the beginning of the rest of my life. It was my new beginning. God has shown me grace and given me another chance to see what being in a happy marriage was all about.

Many people look at turning 40 as the start on the road to the end. They see it as a sign that their life is going downhill. It was the exact opposite for me. I was experiencing joy and peace at a time in my life that the world says I should be looking toward the end. According to Haggai 2:9, the Lord says, *"my latter will be greater than my former."* I remember how it was to be a young bride, and it was a completely different feeling and experience than the one God had given me in my marriage to Kenneith.

I am so thankful that God has brought Kenny into my life. He is a good man, and I know how blessed I am to be his wife. I used to think he would save me from all the things I was running from and help me be a better me. When two people become one flesh, they are there to motivate and encourage each other to be better. That's true. **However**, expecting another person to fix all the things wrong with you or depending on them to make you better is too much pressure. It's unfair to place that type of burden on another human being. None of us has the power to "make" another person better. That's something only God can do.

I saw Kenny as my cure. I believed that marrying him was the answer to me being better than I was before. Yes, marrying him was the start of me not making the same mistakes I'd made in the past, but he wasn't my "cure." With him, I could be better because he showed me pure, unconditional love. He helped me to look in the mirror and see all the amazing things about myself. Most importantly, he constantly reminded me that I am the daughter of the King.

I was no longer the woman who kept marrying the wrong man. With him, I'd make better life decisions because saying yes to being his wife was the first yes of many to come. How had it taken me so long to get here? I felt like all my life had been a dress rehearsal for this moment. I'd completed practice runs in preparation for such a time as this. No, this marriage nor Kenny were a cure to right all my past wrongs, but I found they both directed me back to God: **THE CURE.**

Tyria D. Jones

Releasing the Passion

What is your **passion**? What's the one thing that excites you? If you didn't have to work or be concerned with finances, what's the one thing you'd love to do for the rest of your life? Passion is that thing you can't see yourself *NOT* doing. It's the thing that's always going to be a part of you; what you turn to when everything else is gone. Passion is defined as *"an intense desire or enthusiasm for something."* What is that thing for you?

I grew up journaling and writing down my thoughts. It was the one thing I could control in my life when everything around me was chaotic. I turned to journaling when I was a little girl trying to drown out the thoughts of hating myself. Putting my thoughts on paper was my go-to when I couldn't utter the words aloud. It was my safe place when a physical one didn't exist. I've always loved journals (the prettier, the better). It's like an instant attraction when I see one, and I must make myself **NOT** buy it. We have a built-in bookshelf in our home, and one of the shelves is filled with my journals.

Writing has always come so natural to me. It's like a part of my DNA. I couldn't imagine my life without doing it. It's something I've always been passionate about. Reading is another thing I've always loved to do. Books have been like best friends when I didn't have any. It was my way of escaping into another place and going to other lands. I had a difficult childhood, so reading and journaling were my ways to escape everything around me. I could easily go to other places in my mind and forget about the real things I was experiencing. The characters in the books became like family, and I couldn't wait to see them each day as I entered the stories.

That may sound weird to you, but I've since realized that being a writer has **always** been in me. It's something God placed inside me before my conception. He knew it would be something that would comfort me during times of adversity. He also knew it would be one of the things He'd use to help me minister to others. The gifts and talents God places inside us are for our own enjoyment, but they're also for us to use them to share with the world. When we share them with the world, we direct others back to Him.

Sometimes, we mistakenly think our gifts and talents are just for us; to do with them as we please. Instead of seeking God to find out how we can use them to further His Kingdom, we search for ways to use them to benefit us personally. Yes, I could write books that would help me to gain major exposure, fame, and even lots of money, but what good is that if I'm not helping others? On the other hand, if I get these things while I'm helping others, that's the upside to living for God and being obedient to my calling.

I said it before: ***God doesn't waste ANY experiences.*** He uses them all to work together for our good. In the same way, we must not waste the gifts and talents He's blessed us with. We must honor our calling. What I mean is that once we know the things God has given us to use for our ultimate purpose, it's our responsibility to be good stewards with them.

"When someone has been given much, much will be required in return; and when someone has been entrusted with much, even more will be required."
Luke 12:48

We are here to serve God and to do His will. That includes using everything He's equipped us with to do so.

Once you discover that "thing" that brings you joy, peace, and even comfort while doing it, you **know** it's the one thing that will always be with you. No matter what was going on at different times in my life, I knew I could go back to my writing. God has used it to bring joy, peace, and comfort into my life as I see how He has used my words to help others on their journey. When I think about all the times I could sit down and write, He would speak to me through those words to let me know that is my "thing." It's the one thing I can never release. It's my way of sharing me and who I am with the world, all while being okay with my transparency.

Have you taken time to sit down in your quiet time and reflect on who you are? What do you need to do to find that "thing" inside you? Take a few moments to write down the first things that come to your mind. What do you *LOVE* to do? List those things on the following page. Remember: Your list doesn't have to look like anyone else's. You're unique, and those things are specific to who you are. Once you've completed the list, take it to God and pray over it for the next seven days. Ask Him to give you clarity about those things and what He has given you to help you on the path to fulfilling your purpose for the Kingdom.

TIME FOR REFLECTION
What are you passionate about?

Purpose

When we think about purpose, many things can come to mind. The word means different things to each of us. What does it mean to you? According to Google, purpose is defined as *"the reason for which something is done or created or for which something exists."*

"Thou art worthy, O Lord, to receive glory and honour and power: for Thou hast created all things, and for Thy pleasure they are and were created."
Revelation 4:11

Not only were we created for His pleasure and His will; He gave us something special to do.

For most of my life, I struggled to figure out who I was and why I was here. I looked for the answers in people and situations. Whenever someone would ask me to describe myself, I'd start by saying, *"I'm [his] wife and their mother."* That was my entire identity. I didn't know life any other way. Many times, we identify with our titles instead of who we were created to be. Yes, I was a wife and mother, but that wasn't everything about me. I was more than those things.

When you don't know why you exist, it's easy to start attaching yourself to things because that's what you know. You allow others to tell you who you are, and you try to fill the slots they've placed you in. During times of uncertainty, instead of seeking God for any answers to lingering questions you have, you go to those around you. When you are a person who isn't grounded in your identity, you're a perfect target for others to use for their own desires.

That is one of the reasons it was so easy for my ex-husband to break me down and rebuild me into the person he thought I should be. I allowed him to strip me of my power! Once I submitted to him, I no longer had my own voice, thoughts, desires, or ideas. I looked to him for everything, including telling me who I was. When our relationship began, I was already broken from the turmoil that had occurred in my life before him. By the time he came along, I was "ripe for the picking." What I mean is that I was primed and ready to be his victim. I willingly stepped into the role of the abused woman.

When you grow up being victimized by man after man, you become accustomed to it being your way of life. It's what you expect, so you don't look for anything different. The victim mentality already existed in my mind, so I lived my life on autopilot, conforming to whoever desired to change me. Having someone tell you what to do and how to live your life is a sad way to live. There are no thoughts of your own dreams; no wishes for future things because none of those decisions belong to you.

Once I was able to escape the life of a victim and walk into my freedom, I began to search the scriptures to see what God said about me. I had been told many times that my past didn't determine my future. So many people had reassured me my destiny was in God's hands—not my ex-husband's. I had options! I could choose who I wanted to be and not just accept what my circumstances told me I should be. I didn't have to identify with the labels that had been tacked to my back. I didn't have to be a twice-divorced single mother with no hopes and dreams for the rest of my life.

Instead, I could walk into this new life with hope for a brighter future. My destiny was ahead of me and held many promises. God's Word told me I am royalty and the daughter of the King. Since I am a member of the royal family, I have power. That power comes from my Heavenly Father.

You have that same power! You have the power to choose your destiny and walk in it without fear or trembling! We don't have to apologize for who we are because our status comes with a position in the Kingdom. Once I realized the authority I possessed, I started seeing myself in a different light. I no longer shrunk away and allowed others to define me. I began to define my own purpose. I knew that ability came from God and not people. A woman is the most powerful being when she knows who she is. Those who encounter her will see they can no longer use her for their own selfish desires.

I used to feel like I was a magnet for those who wanted to use and abuse me. I didn't understand how I kept ending up in those same types of relationships. It wasn't just the intimate relationship, but also friendships and those to whom I was acquainted. It seemed as if I had a target on my back. I couldn't comprehend why. What was it about me that told others I could be used and abused? Why did I surrender myself to them without putting up a fight? When you don't realize you have power given to you from your Father, your life is less about pleasing Him and more about pleasing friends, family, and those who cross your path.

> *"We must obey God rather than men."*
> **Acts 5:29**

If we want to be pleasing to God, we must know who God desires us to be. We can't submit to the authority of human beings and not allow God to be the ruler of our lives. He is our Creator and has a unique plan for our lives. Have you sought Him to find out what your purpose is? God knew us before we were formed in our mother's womb, so we existed with Him before that time. Not only did we commune with Him; He created a job specifically for each of us to fulfill for the Kingdom. He knew what it would take for us to reach the point when we'd be ready to walk in that purpose.

Undoubtedly, we each experience good, bad, and ugly moments in our lives, but God uses them to help us on our journey of becoming the woman He designed us to be. He doesn't waste any of it; it all works together for our good because we love Him and are called according to His purpose.

When I think about my life before I knew who I was, I have no regrets. I used to wish I hadn't gone through most of the things I've encountered throughout my life, but I now understand that it was all a part of His ultimate plan for me to get me to where I am today. How could I inspire someone else and tell them they can make it through the pain if I've never felt their pain? How could I help them be a better version of themselves if I hadn't seen the ugliness inside myself? Yes, I know there are times God gives us ways to help others without the personal experiences, but I believe it is more powerful when we can tell another woman how she can overcome because of those experiences. It's not enough to tell her; we must show her what we did to become a conqueror. It's important that we not only focus on ourselves. We must find a way to help others who may come behind us. Our journey isn't just about us; it's for us to help others along the way! I've found that I'm the happiest when I'm helping others. That's when you know you're fulfilling your purpose and doing what God called you to do.

Is there something God has been leading you to do? Do you feel like that thing is too much? Maybe you don't feel capable. I've often heard the saying, *"God doesn't call the qualified; He qualifies the called."* Whatever it is that He has for each of us to do, He has placed people in our path to help us fulfill our purpose. Whatever we're lacking, He will provide in the time we need it. There have been many times I've felt I couldn't "do," but He always sent what I needed.

Whatever it is that you are feeling led to do, seek God for confirmation. It's not something that will come as a surprise to you because **it's already inside of you!**

TIME FOR REFLECTION
What has God placed on your heart to do?

Tyria D. Jones

Say It Loud

Sometimes, we do things and don't really understand why. It isn't until we reflect on them that the answers may come. When we want to change a behavior or an attitude about something, we must dig deep. It's during those times that we must explore all avenues. We often have certain reactions to things and go through life thinking it's normal when, in contrast, it's the opposite of what we should be doing.

I've never understood why security is so important to me. I don't mean security as in having an alarm system for my home. Not in that way. What I'm referring to is the security that is sought in relationships. I've never questioned why I reacted a certain way when I encountered different situations in my marriage—until I kept coming back to the same crossroads. Doing the same thing over and over and expecting a different result is the very definition of insanity.

In my quest toward complete healing, I've chosen to face things head-on. **No more running!** That's the best way to live a life of joy. No more stumbling over things that used to trip me up. I've decided to stop looking backward because there's no longer anything in my past for me. Have you ever said something and stopped midway through your sentence because you don't know why those words just came out of your mouth? That's how it was for me one day when I was having a disagreement with Kenny.

With everything in me, I felt the point I was trying to make was a valid one. Our disagreement was about me needing him to hear me. I was upset because I felt he wasn't listening to the things I was trying to express to him. As I heard myself say the words, I realized:

This wasn't about him; it was about *ME!*

I had brought past things into the present. The fact is that Kenny has always listened to me and allowed me the freedom to use my voice. There has never been a time in our relationship or marriage when I felt he wanted to stifle me or force me into silence. Communication is huge in our relationship! He has always made sure I knew how valuable my voice is to him.

Most of my life, I had no voice. The old saying, *"Children are to be seen and not heard,"* was a **reality** in my childhood. That saying had more to do with children being respectful and not insert themselves into adult conversations. My silence was due to my voice being stripped away by people who should've encouraged me to use my voice. They should've motivated me to be bold and brave; not afraid to speak up for myself. Instead, they forced me to remain silent during times when I should've felt comfortable enough to speak up. It was as if they had placed a muzzle over my mouth to ensure I didn't spill everything that was inside. I was, in essence, placed on "mute." The words continued to elude me well into adulthood. It was the silence that remained when my ex-husband began to abuse me. Again, I didn't feel I could use my voice, so I stayed in the silent abyss.

Although silence became a close friend, I resented all the things it stripped from me. All the times I wanted to leave it once and for all, I was chained to it. The times I wanted to scream, I couldn't. The times I wanted to say, "No, you can't do this to me," I didn't dare give voice to that! There were so many instances when I wanted to use my voice to defend myself, but I couldn't.

There's something about not being able to hear your own voice for so long. Once you get the opportunity to do so, you never want to stop talking. You make sure everyone hears you, whether they want to or not. That was one of the things that attracted me to Kenny. He's not a man of many words, but the words he did say were always comforting, reassuring, and safe. I've always known that I am safe with him. There's security in knowing you can use your voice without facing repercussions.

Sometimes, I mistakenly reach back to pull something from my past. There are moments when I forget I'm no longer muted. I forget I have the freedom to talk, to speak, to shout, and even scream if I want to do so. It's during those times when the memories come flooding in, and I can't distinguish between the past and present. I'm thankful that at those times, Kenny is patient with me.

"Death and life are in the power of the tongue…"
Proverbs 18:21

God has given me the ability to encourage and empower others by using my voice. He has blessed me with the ability to speak life into those around me. He has shown me that my voice is important and needs to be heard by the world. I will never again allow anyone to silence me!

Maybe it wasn't abuse that caused you to be stripped of your voice. Whatever it is, decide today that it's time for you to take your voice back!

Queen Mantra

I'm a Queen and deserve better.
I am strong, brave, and beautiful.
NOW is the time to escape the F.I.R.E.;
To embrace the amazing things waiting for me.
Giving up is not an option. I can do this!

Free at Last

Google defines victory as *"the overcoming of an enemy."* Another definition for it is *"success."* What is your idea of a victorious life? How do you measure success? Some people look at the material things they've accumulated, while others feel it's found in their professional achievements. Sadly, some never find the true meaning of what it means to live a victorious life. It's not found in possessions or positions; it's more about being in the place where God is.

"But seek ye first the Kingdom of God, and His righteousness; and all these things shall be added unto you."
Matthew 6:33

When we seek God first and desire to do what He placed us here to do, then He will provide us with all the things, positions, and whatever else we desire to have. I've experienced this for myself.

All the years I sought after relationships instead of seeking Him, I always came up feeling empty. There were days when I thought a new car or different home would fill the void I felt. I chased after those things until I realized where my true fulfillment would come from, and that peace came when I finally decided to rest in God.

Although you hear others say it or you read it in the Bible, it isn't until you try it for yourself that you know you've found something that is irreplaceable. There truly is victory in Jesus! How do you find it? The moment you decide to surrender your past, present, and future to Him is when you know you're on the right path.

When we come to a place where we can look back at the past things we've experienced and use them to minister to others, that's when we know we're free of those chains. We're no longer bound by the things that used to haunt us. We can walk with our heads held high and know that whatever may come, God's got us.

I recall the first time I was able to share my testimony with someone else. I realized it didn't just help her, but me as well. Every time I can see another woman delivered and set free from her past, it brings my heart joy. I've dedicated my life to empowering women to be the best version of themselves so that they, too, can live a life of victory and strength.

Each of us is meant to share our testimony and say it loudly. The more we speak our truths, the more we will see chains being broken and each person we encounter walking in freedom. Each of us has a story to share. It's time for you to share yours! What are you holding back? What is it about your life that can help someone else be loosed from bondage? Let's not allow fear to stop us from being bold and brave. What can you do today that will change a life tomorrow? Yes, we're all afraid to be transparent, but if it is what God requires, trust that He has a plan.

> *"For I know the plans I have for you, declares the Lord,*
> *plans to prosper you and not to harm you,*
> *plans to give you hope and a future."*
> **Jeremiah 29:11**

Queen, you are **brave**! You are **bold**! You are **beautiful**! You can do all God has called you to do! There's a whole world full of people waiting for you to walk in your greatness, so do it without fear or trembling. You've got this!

I hope that my story has motivated you to let go of the past and walk confidently into your future. Most importantly, I pray it has shown you that everything you need is already inside you. God has equipped you for "such a time as this." It's your time to shine!

F.I.R.E. - The Cycle of Abuse

- **F**ear — Tension is building; you're walking on eggshells, placating him, trying to make sure you don't do anything to upset him.
- **I**ncident — Something happens that angers the abuser; he explodes and you're back in the ugly place.
- **R**emorse — Abuser apologizes, promises not to do it again; you see how sorrowful he is, and he is forgiven; then, he presents gifts.
- **E**xpectation — Honeymoon stage; you're hopeful; things are back to normal or better than normal; you expect it never to happen again.

If your house is on **F.I.R.E**, do you stay inside, or do you **GET OUT** to keep from getting burned or dying?

If you are contemplating whether it's time for you to leave, there's no time like NOW. You keep telling yourself that it'll get better or he'll change. We must remember that none of us can change another human being; only our Heavenly Father can do that. It is only for us to pray for them. Decide today to choose YOU!

You have the power to change your life!
You have the power to determine what your future looks like!
You have the power to determine who you want to be!
You have the power to take control and walk into your destiny with your head held high!

"You are altogether beautiful, my darling; there is no flaw in you."

Song of Solomon 4:7

Resources

Following are resources that will help you along the way to gain strength, clarity, and direction as you continue your journey toward freedom. You will find that the more you fight for the woman God has created you to be, she will emerge with a desire to live victoriously. Once you are truly set free from the chains that have you bound, there will be a burning desire within you to thrive! I pray this list of resources helps on your path to the strong daughter of the King you were born to be.

Hotlines
- ❖ National Domestic Violence Hotline
    - o 1-800-799-7233
- ❖ Texas Department of Family and Protective Services
    - o 1-800-252-5400
- ❖ Childhelp National Child Abuse Hotline
    - o 1-800-422-4453

Emergency/Immediate Assistance
- ❖ Houston Area Women's Center (HAWC)
    - o Emergency Shelter
    - o Legal & Financial Assistance
    - o Counseling, Educational, Housing, and Children's Services
    - o Hotline: 713-528-2121
- ❖ Northwest Assistance Ministries' Family Violence Center
    - o Emergency Services
    - o Legal & Financial Assistance

- Housing, Support, Educational and Children's Services
- Counseling
- Hotline: 281-885-4673
- ❖ Daya
  - Emergency Services
  - Legal & Financial Assistance
  - Counseling
  - Support, Housing & Community Educational Services
  - Hotline: 713-981-7645

Legal Assistance
- ❖ Aid to Victims of Domestic Abuse
  - Legal Services
  - Protective orders, divorce & custody
  - 713-224-9911
- ❖ Gulf Coast Legal Foundation
  - Legal Services
  - Protective orders, divorce & custody
  - 713-652-5911
- ❖ United Way
  - Help Line: 211 (Texas)
- ❖ Public Library
  - Access online help sites
  - https://www.hba.org/domestic-violence-services
- ❖ Woman Inc
  - Affordable housing program for women leaving abusive situations

- Provides an environment where women live independent, violence-free lives
            - Contact: 713-869-9727
            - Email: Info@WOMANInc.us
            - Website: http://www.womaninc.us/
    - ❖ BakerRipley
        - Educational services
            - Pre-k – 8th grade
            - Afterschool programs
        - Enrichment classes
        - Job connections via Workforce Solutions
        - Tax Centers & Financial Services
        - Citizenship & Immigration Services

Book:
- ❖ *A Crown of Beauty for Ashes*
    - Tyria D. Jones
    - TyriaDJones.com
- ❖ *A Crown of Beauty for Ashes 31-day devotional*
    - Tyria D. Jones
    - Email Tyria D. Jones @ tyriadjones@outlook.com to receive
- ❖ *I'm Not Good Enough…and Other Lies Women Tell Themselves*
    - Sharon Jaynes
- ❖ *So Long, Insecurity*
    - Beth Moore
- ❖ *Beautiful in God's Eyes*
    - Elizabeth George
- ❖ *Woman, Thou Art Loosed*
    - T.D. Jakes

About the Author

Tyria D. Jones was born and raised in Pompano Beach, Florida. She is the wife to the love of her life, Kenneith, mother of eight amazing children, and grandmother of five beautiful grandchildren. She is also a Two-Time Bestselling Author, Certified Life Purpose Coach, and Motivational Speaker. She served in the U.S. Army for six years and went on to earn a Bachelor's Degree in Business Management.

Tyria struggled most of her life with finding out who she was; therefore, she lacked self-love. This led her to an abusive relationship/marriage. She lived a life of fear for almost 20 years of her life until one day, she realized she was created for greater things. Today, she dedicates her life and personal story to fulfill God's purpose of helping other women to heal, live a joyous life, love themselves, and walk in their purpose.

In 2016, Tyria captured the attention of women across the country when she wrote her memoir, *A Crown of Beauty for Ashes*. Within, she shared her personal journey from surviving an abusive marriage and homelessness to living a life of victory in God.

The idea to begin a writing career with her own personal experiences came from her husband, Kenneith, planting a seed that encouraged her to be brave and speak boldly about what God had done in her life. Tyria has a desire to encourage, support, and motivate women enduring the same struggles. She is passionate about empowering women to be the best version of themselves so that they, too, can live a victorious life.

Other works by Tyria D. Jones include the *Broken Chains* anthology and the *Soul to Soul* anthology, as well as a companion 31-day devotional for *A Crown of Beauty for Ashes*.

Contact Tyria D. Jones

Email: tyriadjones@outlook.com

Website: tyriadjones.com

Facebook: www.facebook.com/authortyriadjones

Instagram: www.instagram.com/tyriadjones

Appendix

Huffington Post
https://www.huffingtonpost.com/2014/10/23/domestic-violence-statistics_n_5959776.html
30 Shocking Domestic Violence Statistics That Remind Us It's An Epidemic
Alanna Vagianos
10/23/2014 09:25 am ET Updated Dec 06, 2017

US Domestic Violence Murder Rate Rises
Karen Lissner
2019
https://www.ozy.com/acumen/us-domestic-violence-murder-rate-rises/89868

"Why Doesn't She Just Leave?" Barriers to Getting out of Abusive Relationships
Jennifer Focht, MA, National Center for Health Research
http://www.center4research.org/doesnt-just-leave-barriers-getting-abusive-relationships/

Centers for Disease Control and Prevention. National Vital Statistics Reports. Available at http://www.cdc.gov/nchs/data/nvsr/nvsr61/nvsr61_07.pdf . Accessibility verified March 13, 2013.

Bureau of Justice Statistics. Intimate Partner Violence in the U.S. Available at http://www.bjs.gov/content/intimate/victims.cfm. Accessibility verified March 13, 2013.

Co-dependency. https://www.mentalhealthamerica.net/co-dependency. Mental Health America. 2019

Townsend, C., & Rheingold, A.A., (2013). Estimating a child sexual abuse prevalence rate for practitioners: studies. Charleston, S.C., Darkness to Light. Retrieved from www.D2L.org.

www.ingramcontent.com/pod-product-compliance
Lightning Source LLC
Chambersburg PA
CBHW072012110526
44592CB00012B/1281